Wallace Nesbitt, William Henry Beatty

The Boards of Trade General Arbitrations Act (1894)

And Rules of the Toronto Chamber of Arbitration - With Notes and

Suggestions as to the Conduct of a Reference

Wallace Nesbitt, William Henry Beatty

The Boards of Trade General Arbitrations Act (1894)
And Rules of the Toronto Chamber of Arbitration - With Notes and Suggestions as to the Conduct of a Reference

ISBN/EAN: 9783337157807

Printed in Europe, USA, Canada, Australia, Japan

Cover: Foto ©Suzi / pixelio.de

More available books at **www.hansebooks.com**

THE

BOARDS OF TRADE

General Arbitrations Act
(1894)

AND

RULES OF THE TORONTO CHAMBER OF ARBITRATION

WITH

NOTES AND SUGGESTIONS AS TO THE CONDUCT OF A REFERENCE.

BY

W. H. BEATTY.
SOLICITOR TO THE TORONTO BOARD OF TRADE,

AND

WALLACE NESBITT,
OF OSGOODE HALL, ESQUIRES, BARRISTERS-AT-LAW.

———→•←———

Toronto:
HUNTER, ROSE & COMPANY.
1894

CONTENTS.

PAGE.

Table of Cases - - - - - - ii-iii

PART I.

The Boards of Trade General Arbitrations Act (1894) - 1-50

PART II.

Appendix A.—Rules and Forms - - 51-73

B.—Time Table - - - - 75

TABLE OF CASES.

PAGE

Albon *v.* Pike... 11

Allinson *v.* General Council of Medical Education and Registration 11

Attorney-General *v.* Southampton 12

Anning *v.* Hartlet.. 21

Balfour *v.* Malcolm... 11

Baring & Co. *v.* Doulton & Co................................ 11

Ball *v.* Crompton Corset Co 45

Bos *v.* Helsham 33

Beck *v.* Jackson... 45

Beddington *v.* Deitchman..................................... 44

Beddow *v.* Beddow.. 41

Blanchard *v.* Sun & Fire Office.............................. 28

Brook *v.* Delcomyn 14

Carus-Wilson *v.* Greene 6

Carlisle *re* Clegg *v.* Clegg................................ 40

Chadwick *v* Ball... 11

Conmee *v.* C.P.R... 10

Christopher *v.* Hoxon.. 44

Dawdy *re* 6

Dawkins *v.* Antorbus... 5

Duke of Beaufort and Swansea Harbor Trustees *re* 19

East & West India Dock Co. *v.* Krik & Kandell............... 28

Essery *v.* Court Pride....................................... 5

Farrar *v.* Cooper.. 41

Fox *v.* Toronto & Nipissing Ry. Co........................... 44

Frankenburg *v.* The Guarantee Co............................. 11

Groom *v.* Gore... 17

Gunn *v.* Hallett... 29

Hartley *v.* Harker... 12

Hopper *re.* 23

Jacobs *v.* Brett... 11

James *v.* James 28

Jewell *v.* Christie.. 19

Johnson *v.* Latham... 19

Jones *v.* Godson... 20

PAGE

Joplin v. Postlethwaite.. 40
Kemp v. Rose.. 10
Keighley & Co. and Bryant & Co., re....................... 13
Knight and Tabernacle Bldg. Society re................... 39
Lawrence v. Hodgsou.. 18
Lock v. Vulliamey.. 18
London & Blackwell Ry. Co. v. Cross..................... 41
Malmesbury Ry. Co. v. Budd............................... 41
Mosely v. Simpson... 28
McLean v. Evans.. 44
N. London Ry. Co. v. G. N. Ry. Co...................... 41
Nott v. Nott.. 21, 22
Omichund v. Barber.. 34
Oram v Breary... 11
Pappa v. Rose.. 13
Pescod v. Pescod.. 55
Phipps v. Ingram.. 14
Radford v. McDonald... 30
Rees v. Waters... 18
Rennie v. Utterson.. 29
Ross v. Boards.. 21
Stonehewer v. Farrar.. 17
Southampton Bridge Co. v. Southampton Local Board...... 12
Tandy v. Tandy... 20
Talbot v. Poole... 44
Tharsis Sulphur Co. v. Loftus.............................. 13
Thorburn v. Barnes.. 14
Turnock v. Sartoris.. 40
Tunno v. Bird... 56
Vineberg v. Guardian Fire and Life Insurance Co....... 10
Wakefield v. Llanelly.. 18
Whiteby v. Roberts... 28
Whitworth v. Hulse.. 19
Williams v. Squair.. 23
Wallis v. Hirsch.. 40
Workingmen's Mutual Society re............................ 44
Wilson & Sons and Eastern Counties Navigation and Trans-
 port Co. (Limited) re... 12
Young v. Bulman... 55

ERRATA.

On page 11, line 4, for "burglar," read *burglary*.

On page 11, line 6 from bottom, for "decision," read *dictum*.

On page 20, S. 2, for "Form of," read *Taking up*,

On page 32, line 22, for "subpœna," read *summons*.

On page 33, for "Bass *v* Helsham," read *Bos v. Helsham*.

On page 57, Rule 14, last line, after "Form M.", add *or Form M.2.*

On page 62, Rule 22, after "Form M.", add *Form M.2.*

THE

BOARDS OF TRADE
GENERAL ARBITRATIONS ACT
(1894).

————✦➤✦⬥✦◂✦————

An Act enabling Boards of Trade in Cities to appoint general arbitrators for certain purposes.

(Ont. Statute, 57 Vict., Cap. 24).

The object of the Legislature in the passing of this
Act was to attain the three primary essentials of
justice—cheapness, celerity and certainty. Perhaps
it may be well, before taking up the different provisions in detail, to give a few of the special features of
the Act somewhat at length.

1st. The majority of cases which will be brought
for arbitrament may be finally disposed of in a couple
of hours.

There will be no lingering about courts day after
day waiting for a hearing.

The hour will be fixed beforehand and strictly ad-
hered to. Accommodation will be provided for the
hearing of several cases concurrently, and the panel
of arbitrators will be sufficiently large to do away
with the necessity of waiting the convenience of
judges, or the termination of protracted cases.

Forensic displays will not be encouraged, nor will the practice of cross-examination be permitted to be abused, the conduct of the Chamber being under the control of men of business " anxious to get at facts, and arrive at a common sense conclusion as speedily as may be, with due regard to efficiency."

The hearing of every case is to be continued *de die in diem*.

2nd. With a saving of time, and a simplification of procedure, there will necessarily be a vast reduction in expense, and apart from legal assistance (which is at the option of either of the parties), the whole fees payable to the Chamber, including arbitrator's fees, will not probably exceed $20.00 for each sitting, whatever may be the amount at issue.

3rd. Disputants may conduct their own cases, or be represented by a legal advocate, barrister, solicitor, or by other duly authorized agent. The fees for witnesses will be the same as in an action in a High Court of Justice.

4th. The panel of arbitrators will include representatives of all trades and allied interests, will be nominated by the Council of the Board, and balloted for by the Corporation.

The entire proceedings of the Chamber will be considered strictly private and confidential, the parties and their agents alone being present, and no reports being issued.

5th. The submission to arbitration once made (whether in the original contract between the parties, or by a special agreement *ad hoc*), it cannot be revoked, nor is it affected by the death of either of the partics ; and the arbitrators may proceed in the absence of any party who, after reasonable notice, shall neglect or refuse to attend on a reference.

Witnesses may be examined on oath, and the parties must produce all documents in their possession or control which the arbitrators may call for.

The personal attendance of all parties may be dispensed with if they prefer to jointly state a case, on which they agree to accept the decision of the arbitrator.

The rules further provide for an impartial legal assessor, to whom any question of construction of documents, or admissibility or relevancy of evidence, or other legal question, may be referred by the parties or arbitrators for their guidance, thus safeguarding the parties by the advantage of practically an inexpensive judicial determination of matters, and avoiding the necessity of procuring legal advocacy to guard against departure from legal and judicial rules.

The advantages of this are so obvious in inexpensively settling disputes, no matter how large the sum involved, as to require no comment.   It may be proper to say, however, that in England it has been found productive of the greatest benefits, ensuring as it does the disposition of cases as satisfactorily as if tried before one of the courts without the necessity of the enormous expense of litigants having to retain solicitors and counsel to advocate their views.

The Chamber gives trained experts or practical business men, with power to call in trained impartial legal assistance where necessary.

The award of the arbitrators may be enforced in

the same manner as a judgment or order of the High
Court of Justice to the same effect, so that there are
at least five different advantages which the Chamber
offers over the ordinary methods and remedies :

(*a*) A convenient place for hearing, with all the
machinery of a court.

(*b*) Carefully adjusted rules of procedure, which
will act as a guide to disputants.

(*c*) A selected, efficiently organized panel of
arbitrators.

(*d*) A regulated moderate scale of fees.

(*e*) The assistance of a *special* " Legal Assessor "
to sit with the arbitrator or arbitrators, and
advise and assist him or them in the arbitration.

This Act in no way interferes with the special Act
incorporating the Board of Trade, and the rules made
thereunder. The distinction between an arbitration
held under that Act and the rules established thereunder, and an arbitration under this Act, is a broad one.
In the case of arbitrations under the Board of Trade
rules, the By-laws provide for the members being
bound to abide by the arbitrament, and in case of
refusal to obey the award, machinery is provided for
complaint to be made to the Secretary of the Board,
who then brings the matter before the Council, and
unless the recalcitrant member complies with the
order of the Council, provision is made for his expul-
sion from all the privileges of the Board and forfeiture
of his seat. This penalty is, of course, entirely in-
applicable to ordinary arbitration between parties,
and by Section 33 of this Act, it is provided that it

is in no way intended to interfere with the provisions of the Act, relating to the Toronto Board of Trade, or the arbitration between members thereof held under such Acts and rules. The class of cases applicable to arbitrations held under the Board of Trade rules are those relating to Clubs and Benefit Societies, in which it has been held that the members submit themselves to any disqualifying provisions which may exist, always providing that they are not contrary to the rules of natural justice. See Dawkins v. Antrobus, L.R. 17 Ch. D. 615; Essery v. Court Pride, 2 O.R. 596.

WHEREAS the Board of Trade of the City of Toronto has been enabled to procure the settlement of differences between the members of their corporation by arbitration with unusual economy and despatch; and whereas the said Board of Trade has resolved that in the opinion of the Board the success attendant on their system of arbitration justifies its extension to persons or corporations other than members of the Board; and whereas it is desirable to give effect to the experience of the said Board, and to extend such system aforesaid and its advantages to other cities where Boards of Trade have been established, in case such boards desire to avail themselves of this Act; *Preamble.*

Therefore Her Majesty, by and with the advice and consent of the Legislative Assembly of the Province of Ontario, enacts as follows:

1. This Act may be cited as *The Boards of Trade General Arbitrations Act, 1894.* *Short title.*

Arbitration, What is?

A broad distinction exists between an arbitrator and a valuator. In the case of an arbitrator, he is presumed to perform judicial functions; in the case of a valuator, he is presumed simply to be appointed by the party to use his own judgment, and by the exercise of his knowledge and his senses to come to a conclusion, and the rules relating to arbitrations do not apply. See In. *re* Dawdy, L.R., 15 Q.B.D. 426; In *re* Carus-Wilson v. Greene, L.R., 18 Q.B.D. 7 (1887).

Another broad distinction between an arbitration and valuation is, in case of parties agreeing that a certain thing is to be decided by a valuator, then in case such person named refuses to act or dies, the parties are powerless; whereas, in the case of arbitration, the rule (17a) provides that the registrar may nominate an arbitrator; in other words, in the case of valuation, it is impossible for a party to obtain specific performance of a contract without first obtaining valuation; the Court cannot put itself in the place of a valuator and arrive at a decision.

Parties to Arbitration.

Any number of persons may join in a submission, and provided the arbitrator does not go outside the subject matter of the submission, he may decide their joint and several rights and liabilities, including questions of contribution.

Corporations may refer their disputes to arbitration by submission under seal. Partners may refer their partnership disputes or their disputes with third parties to arbitration. But all the partners must join, unless otherwise provided for by their deed or agreement or articles of partnership.

An agent has generally no authority to bind his principal by a submission, but if he has authority to compound debts or settle claims, he may refer such matters to arbitration.

An infant is not bound by his submission, unless it be made with the sanction and approval of the Court, as a proceeding beneficial to him.

A lunatic would not be bound; but his committee may, by the permission of the Court, bind his estate by a submission.

Matters to be referred.

These should be stated with sufficient clearness, otherwise inconvenient questions may arise as to what is and what is not within the jurisdiction of the arbitrators.

A reference of " all matters of difference " will give the arbitrators jurisdiction over all disputes which have arisen between the parties down to the date of the submission, but not over matters contingent or which arise after the date of submission. If the parties wish to submit contingent or future differences they may do so, but this must be stated in the submission.

If disputes between partners are referred, and it is desired to give the arbitrators power to decide whether or not the partnership should be dissolved, and in case of a dissolution to take the accounts of the partnership and decide the respective rights of the partners, this should be expressly stated. The same particularity should be observed when one of the matters in dispute is the construction of the partnership deed. If it is intended by one of the parties to raise an issue of fraud, so that the reputation of both or either of the parties may depend on the result of the arbitration, it will not be desirable to rely only on the form " all matters in difference," but to state the issue in such a manner that it shall be clear, that at the time of signing the submission the parties knew that the issue of fraud would be raised. These suggestions are made because there is a two-fold advantage to the parties to a submission in having the subject matter of the disputes between them clearly defined. The main object of an arbitration is to avoid any proceeding at law, and to render the award of the arbitrator final. One common means for an arbitration to fail to be final and to come before the courts eventually, is for the arbitrator to give an award about matters which are not expressly included in the written submission, which is the sole foundation of his authority. Even in cases where both parties have been desirous of an arbitration at the outset, and indeed up to the publication of the award, the losing party finds himself dissatisfied, and then searches for a means to prevent the award being acted upon, a search which rarely indeed benefits the seeker and cannot possibly personally benefit the successful party to the award. But there is also a second advantage in a clear definition of the subjects which are to be included in the submission. There have been many cases where one party to a submission has changed his mind before the hearing, and has then declined to proceed with the arbitration, and has instituted an action. It must, therefore, be here pointed out that when a party has commenced an action it is not a defence *per se* for the defendant to say that the plaintiff has already agreed to submit to arbitration the dispute upon which he is now proceeding.

Who may Act as Arbitrator.

In arbitrations between individuals the general law which is applicable is to be found in R.S.O., Cap. 53, as amended by 52 Vic., Cap. 13, passed in 1889, and shortly, the general law may be stated to be that no party can be chosen as an arbitrator who has any pecuniary interest, no matter how small, in the result of the award ; nor can a party be chosen, who, from hostility or bias, is likely to to be influenced in his decision. A few illustrations may be given as to what has been decided.

(1) After the amount of a loss by fire had been ascertained by arbitration, the assured discovered that the company's arbitrator was a sub-agent of the company's district agent. He then refused to abide by the result of the award and was upheld by the court in his refusal.

Vineberg v. Guardian Fire and Life Assurance Company, 19 Ont. A. R. 293.

(2) Where an arbitrator had, during the progress of the arbitration, been approached by one of the parties with reference to accepting a position as solicitor to such party, and was after the award, appointed to that office, the award was set aside.

Conmee v. Canadian Pacific Railway Company, 16 Ont. R. 639.

(3) When a builder bound himself to abide by the decision of an architect as to the amount to be paid for his work, not knowing that the architect had given an assurance that the cost of the work would not exceed a certain sum, although he had refused to guarantee that it would not do so, it was held that the architect was under such a bias as deprived his decision of binding force. Kemp v. Rose, 1 Giff. 258.

(4) Where a dispute on some matter outside the reference had arisen between the arbitrator and one of the parties, it was held that the arbitrator could

not properly act. In the matter of a contract between Baring & Co. and Doulton & Co., 8 Times L. R. 701 (1892).

(5) The manager of a burglar guarantee company is not a fit person to adjust the loss suffered by a subscriber. In the matter of an arbitration between Frankenburg and The Guarantee Company, 10 Times L R. 393 (1894).

(6) See also Allinson vs. General Council of Medical Education and Registration (1894), 1 Q. B. 750.

Objection to arbitrator, how taken :

Under the special Act in this case, if the award has been made it is doubtful if the Court could interfere unless for actual fraud; but relief could be had at any time during the progress of an arbitration by an injunction preventing the arbitrator acting, see under this head, as illustrating the proposition that, although the Court cannot give leave to revoke the submission, it would probably hold that its power to interfere by injunction was not taken away : Oram v. Brearey, 2 Ex. D. 346 (1877), where Pollock, B., says : "The jurisdiction of a Superior Court is not to be ousted unless by express language in, or obvious inference from, some Act of Parliament." See also Chadwick v. Ball, L. R., 14 Q. B D. 855 (1885), where, although the decision in Oram v. Brearey was overruled, the above decision was cited with approval by Lindley L. J., at p 858. See also a statement to the same effect by Jessel, M. R., in Jacobs v. Brett, L. R, 20 Eq Cas. p. 1, at p. 6, (1875); and Tindal, C. J., in Albon v. Pyke (1842), 4 M. & G. 424 ; Lord Campbell in Balfour v. Malcolm (1842), 8 Cl. & F. 485, at p. 500.

In 1777 it was held that a Statute which enacted
that "all offences shall be determined" in a certain
inferior Court did not take from the Court of King's
Bench the power of removing a matter in a proper
case : Hartley v. Hooker, 2 Cowp 523 ; and, in 1849,
that the Court is not ousted of its preventive
jurisdiction to stop by injunction the misapplication
of poor rates, by the power given to the poor law
commissioners by Statute to determine the propriety
of all such expenditure : Attorney-General v. Southampton, 17 Sim. 6. See also : Southampton Bridge
Co v. Southampton Local Board (1858), 8 E. and B.
804 : Maxwell on Statutes (1883), pp. 152 et seq.;
Hardcastle on Statutes (1892), pp. 140, et seq.

But for the special provisions of s. 23 of the Act
in question, there would be three courses open :

(a) Motion to set aside awards.

(b) Motion to revoke submission.

(c) Motion for injunction to prevent arbitrator
acting.   In view of ss. 7 and 23, the latter course
seems to be the only course open where formerly the
usual course was to move to revoke.

This seems the more likely, as the Court will, no
doubt, be astute in the case of an arbitrator who is
biased, etc., to prevent his acting ; and Rule 17
" A " may be invoked as applicable, and the Registrar
directed to appoint a new arbitrator upon the
declaration of the Court that the arbitrator attached
is " incapable of acting."   See : In re an arbitration
between Wilson & Sons and the Eastern Counties
Navigation and Transport Company (Limited), 8
Times L. R. 264 (1892).

Actions Against Arbitrator.

No action can be brought against the arbitrator for want of care and skill in the matter of the reference, provided he has acted honestly : See Pappa v. Rose, L. R. 7 C. P.525 ; Tharsis Sulphur Co. v. Loftus, L. R. 8 C. P.   See also Rule 18, post. p.

Proceedings Before Arbitration.

(1)   *Presence of Counsel.   Rules of Evidence.*

In the case of an arbitration, ordinarily, when it is entered upon, both parties have the right to be represented by Counsel ; see *post* sec. 19, and to call wit nesses, but arbitrators are not bound by the ordinary rules of legal evidence.   See in *re* Keighley & Co., and Bryant & Co., 9 Times L. R. 107, at p. 108.

As to form of oath, see *post* notes under Sec 15 of the Act.

It is not within the scope of the present work to describe fully the rights and limitations of the parties in examining, cross-examining and re-examining wit⁻ nesses ; but it had perhaps better be stated that a party examining a witness in chief can only obtain from him by questions, evidence of matters strictly material to the issue being heard.   Nor can a party examining his own witness ask leading questions, that is, ask questions in such a form as to put the answer into the witness's mouth.   In cross-examination a party may ask questions of an opponent's witness, going to his credit, that is to say, which may show that the witness is not worthy of belief, and this, of course, can be shewn from matters quite extraneous to the question at issue.

The arbitrator or arbitrators have power, and it is their duty, to check any abuse of the rights of cross-examination.

In re-examination the witness can only be asked as to matters "arising out of the cross-examination." Any fresh material which has been forgotten, or was not considered material when the witness was first examined, should be put through the arbitrator, or by his leave, and if the matter is new the opponent should be allowed to cross-examine upon it.

An arbitrator or umpire must not decide against a party without hearing all he has to say, although he may be of opinion that there is nothing the party can bring forward which will alter his opinion. Phipps v. Ingram, 3 Dowl. 669 (1835); Thorburn v. Barnes, L. R. 2 C. P. 384 (1867) This, of course, does not apply when a party refuses or neglects to attend the hearing without reasonable cause, because in that case the party has not given the arbitrator an opportunity of hearing him. Neither does it apply to a case of rejection or evidence which the arbitrator or umpire believes to be legally inadmissible.

An arbitrator or umpire should not hear any evidence in favor of one side privately, because each party has a right to know what is the evidence against him, so that he may refute it if he can. (See Earle J. in re Brook & Delcomyn 16 C. B. N. S. 403. 1864).

(2) *Order of Business.*

The arbitrator has general control over the order of business, but it is well for him to allow the parties to adopt their own order if they can agree upon it.

In most cases there is one party who makes a claim and another who repudiates it, and in that case it is generally the party claiming who should begin (but see below).

Where there are claims and cross claims to be heard, it will be generally convenient for that party to begin whose claim arises first in order of date, but this is a matter about which no general rule can be profitably laid down.   The common sense of the parties and the arbitrators will generally be sufficient to guide them as to which party should be heard first. In some cases, the facts necessary (*prima facie*) to establish the claim are admitted by the defendant, but he, in defence, sets up a matter which it is his duty to prove if he wishes to succeed in defeating the claim, and in such a case, the defendant who sets up the disputed matter should begin.   (See Case iv. below.)

The easiest method of shewing what is generally the most convenient order to pursue is to give a series of simple examples.

CASE I.—(Claim and Denial.)

A. claims $50 against B. for breach of contract. B. denies the breach.

(1)—A. opens his case upon the contract and states what is the breach complained of.

(2)—A. places all his evidence before the arbitrators. The witnesses are cross-examined by B. and re-examined by A.

(3)—B. states what is his defence.

(4)—B. places all his evidence before the arbitrators, etc., as in 2.

(5)—B. sums up the whole case.

(6)—A. replies upon the whole case.

If B. does not intend to give evidence or call witnesses, but relies wholly on the weakness of A.'s case, then substitute.

(3)—A sums up on the case.

(4)—B. sums up on the case.

CASE II.—(Claim and cross-claim where the subject matters are mixed.)

A. claims $100 against B. for goods sold. B. disputes the amount and cross-claims for a breach of warranty.

(1)—A states what is his case as to goods sold.

(2)—A. places his evidence before the arbitrators as to goods sold. B. cross-examines the witnesses as to the amount and the breach of warranty. A. re-examines.

(3)—B. states his view as to the whole dispute.

(4)—B. produces evidence as to the whole dispute. A. cross-examines. B. re-examines witnesses.

(5 A. produces additional evidence (if any) as to breach of warranty.

(6)—B. sums up on whole case.

(7)—A. sums up on whole case.

In this case A. is not called on to state his case or produce his evidence rebutting the breach of warranty until B has closed his case, because he may not know at the outset what is the case set up against him by B as to breach of warranty.

CASE III.—(Claim and cross-claim distinct.)

A. claims $100 against B. for goods sold. B. claims $50 against A. for work done under a contract.

In this case, each claim should be heard separately, as in Case I.

CASE IV.—(When burden of proof is on defendant.)

A. claims $100 against B. for breach of contract by refusing to accept goods. B. admits the contract and the tender of the goods, but says he refused to accept them because they were inferior to sample.

In this case A. is relieved by B.'s admission from having to prove the contract and tender. B. therefore, begins by stating his case as to the goods being inferior to sample, and the order will be the same as in Case I., substituting B. for A. and A. for B.

If any case of difficulty arises, it rests entirely with the arbitrator or arbitrators to decide in what order the parties are to be heard, and the arbitrator or arbitrators have complete control over the conduct of the trial.

(3) *Arbitrator's Notes.*

In Groom vs. Gore (25 L.J. Ex. 267 (1856), the Court said, "The taking of notes upon an arbitration may be necessary, and the proper duty of the arbitrator is to take notes so far as he deems it necessary."

The Award.

(1)—*General Requisites.*

(a) The award must be certain.

There must be no question as to what are the rights and duties of the parties under the award.   In Stonehewer vs. Farrer, 14 L.J., Q.B., 122 (1845,) the arbitrator directed that the defendant should take all necessary precautions to prevent certain water being unfit for the use of the plaintiff. This was held to

be a bad award, because an "award should be so
specific, that a party can have no difficulty in acting
upon it," In Lawrence vs. Hodgson 1 Y. & J. 16
(1826), an award that A. or B. do a certain thing,
without saying which should do it, was held to be bad.
In the same connection, it may be mentioned, that
an award should distinctly shew what the parties are
to do, not what the arbitrator recommends as a
reasonable compromise. In Lock vs. Vulliamey, N.
& M. 336 (1833), an award was held invalid where
the arbitrator said : " To meet the circumstances of
the case in a liberal manner, I propose that Mr. V.
should pay Mr. L. £10."

(b) The award must be final.

The award must be a final settlement of the matters
referred.   In Wakefield vs. Llanelly etc., Co. 12 L.T.
509 (1865), Lord Justice Tumer said, "It is the duty
of arbitrators fully and finally to decide all the
questions which by the agreement of reference are
submitted to their determination, and an award which
disposes of some of those questions and leaves others
of them undecided, or leaves it in doubt as to any of
the questions, whether they were meant to be, and
have been decided, or not been decided, cannot be
maintained."

If one of the matters in difference has been dropped
during the arbitration or has not been brought before
the arbitrators, the award cannot be impeached because such matters are not mentioned therein.   Rees
vs. Waters 16 M. & W. 263 (1847).

When the award professes to be made "of all the
matters referred to," there is a presumption that all

the matters referred have been disposed of, and that the award is an adjudication that there is no other claim maintainable beyond what is expressly stated Jewell vs. Christie 36 L. J., C. P. 168 (1867), and it has been held that where an arbitrator, to whom has been submitted a claim and cross claim, awards a gross sum of money to one party, there is a presumption that he has disposed of both claim and cross claim, although these are not distinguished in the award. *Re* Duke of Beaufort and Swansea Harbor Trustees, 29 L J., C. P. 241 (1860). If the submission requires that the arbitrator shall find separately as to several sums claimed, he must do so, but if the submission does not so require, he may award a lump sum. Whitworth vs. Hulse, L. R. 1 Ex. 251 (1866).

It is the duty of an arbitrator to himself determine by his award the whole matter referred; he should not leave anything to be decided afterwards by the judgment of himself or another. See Johnson vs. Latham 19 L. J., Q. B. 329 (1850). " An arbitrator cannot in his award, reserve either to himself or delegate to another the power of performing in future any act of a judicial nature respecting the matters submitted (Russell on Arbitration, 7th edition, p. 281.) He may, however, direct matters of a purely ministerial character to be done, and if called on to value a property, he may determine the rate to be charged per acre, leaving the acreage to be ascertained by measurement, because measurement is but a ministerial act. The fixing of a value on the other hand is not a ministerial but a judicial act, and should be settled by the arbitrator himself, not left to a third party (*Ib.* pp. 283, 284.)

As an award cannot of itself operate to convey land, it may often be necessary for an arbitrator to direct a conveyance to be made, and if he does so, he should declare who is to bear the expense. He should not leave material question as to covenants or releases to the decision of the draughtsman, nor may he reserve to himself a future power to decide who shall draw the deed. See Tandy vs. Tandy, 9 Dowl., 1044 (1841).

(2)—*Form of Award.*

When the award is made in ordinary practice, the rule is for the arbitrator to notify both the parties when the award is ready for delivery and the amount of his fees, and a claim for more fees than the arbitrators are entitled by law to tax renders them liable under the Statute to a penalty for three times the amount claimed by them. R.S.O., Cap. 53, Sec. 29. A somewhat singular case arose recently where the parties innocently, in giving notice, made demand for larger fees than the Statute allowed, and were sued for the penalties, some $1,500, but so far have escaped on the ground that the award being lodged at a bank, with a notice that the same was to be taken up there, a cheque which was given in payment of the award, was not money, and therefore the arbitrators having discovered their mistake and notified the withdrawal of the demand were held not liable. The case, however is still in appeal. Jones vs. Godson, C.P. Div. Ct. Ont., 23rd June, 1894.

(3) *Costs.*

Costs Part of the Award.

It should be remembered that costs are part of the award. These must be awarded separately and not

as a part of the whole sum of money awarded, otherwise it will not be clear whether or not the arbitrator
has exceeded his jurisdiction as to costs.   An arbitrator may award costs generally, or he may award a
lump sum for costs.   He should state to whom and
by whom the costs are to be paid, and if he intends
that each party shall pay his own costs he should say
so.   (See Post, Sec 28 and notes thereunder.)

(4) *Forms of Award.*

The award must be in writing signed by the arbitrator or arbitrators.   When there are three arbitrators
an award by two of them is sufficient, and a third
arbitrator who dissents from the award will simply
omit to sign his name.   If more than one arbitrator
signs all should sign at the same time and place.   See
Anning v. Hartlet, 27 L.J. Ex. 145 (1858).   Nott v.
Nott, 5 O. R. 280.

It is usual for an award to be attested by one witness, but this is not essential.

It is not essential that there should be any prelim-
inary recitals of fact, but certain recitals are advisable.
So much of the submission should be set forth as will
shew what are the matters referred.   Where applicable, the following recitals are recommended :—The
appointment of a new arbitrator ; the appointment of
a third arbitrator who has entered on the reference ;
the enlargements of time.   It is also advisable to state
that the award has been made "concerning the matters referred."

In stating the terms of the award, technical phraseology need not be employed, but the intention of the
arbitrator must be clearly stated.

If, by the terms of the submission, the arbitrator is
required to find as to certain facts, he must do so ;
otherwise it is not necessary to state the facts on
which the arbitrator has based his decision. Neither
is an arbitrator required to state his reasons for the
award.

If the question is what money (if any) is due on a
contract as debt or damages, he must state the exact
sum awarded, who is to pay it, and to whom it is to
be paid, and within what time, or forthwith. If he
awards lands or chattels, he must describe them so
pecifically that they can be readilyd indentified. If
he directs a certain thing to be done, he should say
how it is to be done and within what time. As to
directing a conveyance of land, see R. S. O., c. 53
s. 45.

<h3 style="text-align:center">(5) Signing the Award.</h3>

In ordinary cases the arbitrators must all be present when the award is signed, and this rule must be
most stringently observed. See Nott v. Nott, 5 Ont.,
Rep. 283 (1884).

In this case three arbitrators, at the close of the
evidence, agreed on their finding, and a minute thereof was made in writing by one of them but not signed,
and it was understood that nothing further was to be
done but to have a formal award drawn up and executed.
Next day the award was drawu up and executed by
two of the arbitrators in the presence of each other,
but in the absence of the third arbitrator, who a couple
of days afterwards executed it in the presence of one
of the other arbitrators. In an action on the award it
was held that the award should have been executed by
the three arbitrators together, and that it was invalid.

But in a case where two arbitrators having agreed on a referee did not both sign the appointment at the same time, it was held that the signing of the appointment, not being a judicial act, had been validly performed, *re* Hopper, L.R. 2 Q.B. 367 (1867).

And where an informal memorandum of the award was signed by all the arbitrators at a meeting, but the arbitrators were not together when signing the formal award, the award was good. Williams vs. Squair, 10 U.C.Q.B. 24 (1852).

Within the limits of a short sketch such as this, it is impossible to indicate. the law on all the phases that may arise, but these are the rules generally governing arbitrations. Under the various sections of the Act will be noted such observations as either amplify these rules or derogate from the general rule by reason of the special Statutory provisions.

2. It shall be the duty of the Council of the Board of Trade of the City of Toronto, hereinafter called "the Board," from time to time to determine the number of persons which, in the opinion of the council, shall be sufficient to form a Chamber of Arbitration, from among whom Boards of Arbitration may be selected to hear and decide controversies, disputes or misunderstandings which may be voluntarily submitted to them for arbitration.

Council of Toronto Board of Trade to determine number of Arbitrators.

It would seem under this Section that the Council of the Board of Trade are compelled to determine simply the number of persons, and, that these persons when elected as provided for in Section 3 are to be

divided into Boards of Arbitration according to the
special qualifications of the persons composing the
Board; that is to say, persons skilled in any particular
trade or manufactory in one board, as in the scheme
in the Board of Trade itself, where the members may
have what are called Sections, such as Bankers' Sections, and Dry Goods Sections, etc., and it would
seem to be intended that the Council should nominate
a certain number of persons representing the various
interests that are likely to require special attention,
and all these persons should be relegated to act in
matters coming within their peculiar knowledge.

The idea of the legislation being, apparently, that by
bringing to bear expert knowledge disputes may be
much more expeditiously disposed of than if a great
deal of evidence had to be offered to practically put
the tribunal disposing of the matter in a position to
know that which the parties themselves would take for
granted in the dealing without anything being said,
and bearing in mind the rule that arbitrators are not
bound by strict rules of evidence, the scheme, if car-
ried out in the apparent spirit of the legislation
would be productive of most beneficial results in disposing of matters shortly. It would seem to be well,
therefore, if the Council would nominate and the
Board appoint Engineers and other skilled experts
who could deal with questions of this kind, without
the necessity of Counsel appearing, and dispose of the
rights of the parties summarily and satisfactorily.

3. (1) The Council shall nominate from the
community generally not less than *thirty*
persons who shall have given their consent in writing to act as arbitrators; out

Nomination
of Persons
to act as
arbitrators.

of which number there shall be elected by ballot
by the members of the Board of Trade at a special meeting called for that purpose the number
so determined upon by the Council as sufficient
to form a Chamber of Arbitration.

(2) Any of the persons so elected may be mem-
bers of the Board of Trade, but such *Electing members of Board of Trade as arbitrators.*
membership shall not be a necessary
qualification of the persons elected.

(3) Immediately after the election a list of the
persons elected shall be published in *The* *List of persons elected to be gazetted.*
Ontario Gazette and such other papers
as the Council of the Board may determine.

(4) The appointment shall be for two years
from the date of the election, provided *Term of office of arbitrators.*
nevertheless that if at the expiration of
two years any arbitration shall be pending before any arbitrator, his appointment so far
as such unfinished business is concerned shall not
be affected until such business is determined.

(5) The names of such boards of arbitrators
shall be continuously posted in the *Names of arbitrators to be kept posted up.*
offices of the Board of Trade in the
Board of Trade building.

(6) Provided that if any person appointed as
aforesaid to act as an arbitrator be *Disqualification of arbitrators.*
convicted of any indictable offence, his
appointment to act as such arbitrator
shall forthwith be vacated, and if such person

at such time is engaged in an arbitration, the other two shall have all the powers of the three to continue such arbitration and make an award.

Under this section the method of calling a special meeting is provided for in the By-laws of the Board of Trade, and compliance with By-law No. 12 would seem to be necessary, and an election held in compliance with that by-law would seem to be sufficient. It is suggested that in the notice calling a special meeting the names of all parties who have consented in writing to act as arbitrators should be set out, and that the meeting be called for the purpose of electing the number which has previously been specified by the Council in a Resolution, as sufficient to form a Chamber of Arbitration.

Sub-Section 3 should be carefully followed, and in the previous proceeding of the Council it should be stated whether publication in the *Ontario Gazette* only should be sufficient, or whether publication should take place in any other papers, naming them, and if not intended to be published in any other papers it should be so stated.

4. The Board of Trade is to provide parties who submit to arbitration under this Act, with arbitration rooms and all necessary forms and papers, and is to Rooms to be provided. do or cause to be done all such acts as they lawfully may do, for the purpose of assisting the parties to the arbitration in the course of the arbitration.

5. The Secretary of the Board shall be *ex-officio* registrar of all arbitrations under this Act, unless the Board make a separate appointment; and the duties of the registrar shall (in addition to any duties which the council of the Board may by rules in writing prescribe) be as follows: He shall receive submission and payment of fees and costs; shall notify the arbitrators and umpire of their appointments: give notice of hearing to parties; issue summons for attendance of witnesses and production of documents; keep a register of submissions, a register of awards and reconciliation, and such other books and memoranda, and make such returns as the council of the Board of Trade shall from time to time require. He shall render such assistance to the arbitrator or arbitrators in the arbitration as he or they may require, and generally shall carry out the instruction of the Board.

Registrar and his duties.

6. All arbitrations under this Act shall be held before one arbitrator, or two or three arbitrators, according to the desire and agreement of the parties.

Number.

7. Parties assenting to an arbitration by an instrument in writing duly executed by them according to the form in Schedule A to this Act, or to that effect, and filing the same with the registrar, shall not be entitled to revoke the submission.

Submission.

This is a change in the law. The Arbitration Act, R.S.O., 1887, Chap. 53, Sec. 16, provided for a judge or court revoking the submission, and such power was

only exercised where the arbitrator had been guilty
of misconduct, or for some reason was unfit to have
the conduct of the reference, and mere circumstances
of suspicion, as where the arbitrator lunched with
one of the parties, would not be sufficient See
Moseley vs. Simpson, L.R. 16, Equity, 226 (1873),
and in re Whiteley vs. Roberts, L. R. (1891) 1 Ch.
558, where it was held that evidence of an admission
by an arbitrator that he had been bribed was not ad-
missible as against the party holding the award.

The Statute, prescribing as it does that the parties
shall not be entitled to revoke, would leave the party
only a remedy in case of inability to prove fraud, or as in
Blanchard vs. Sun & Fire Office, T.Q.R. 395 (1890),
an award was set aside because the arbitrator, before
making it, had acquired the subject matter of the
award. Such cases as the East and West India Dock
Co. vs. Kirk and Kandell, L.R. 12, App. Cas. 738
(1887), and James vs. James, L.R. 23 Q.B.D., p. 12
(1889), will no longer be applicable, where the arbitrator is merely going wrong in law, particularly
when this is read with Section 23 of the Act, and
makes a very great departure from the ordinary rules
of law, and a departure it is conceived in the public
good, because the whole scheme of the Act is an inexpensive and summary disposition of the case.

8. The arbitrators shall after their appointment and before acting in any case as
arbitrators, take and subscribe an oath *Arbitrators to be sworn.*
before a justice of the peace or a com-
missioner for taking affidavits in the High Court
of Justice, that they will faithfully, diligently

and impartially perform their duties as arbitrators, and will, in all cases to be submitted, give a true and just award according to the best of their judgment and ability, without fear, favor or affection of or to any person whomsoever.

9. Arbitrators nominated by the parties under this Act shall, in each case before they act, take and subscribe a similar oath; Oaths. which may be in the form of Schedule B to this Act, and such oath shall be filed with the registrar.

The joint effect of these two sections would seem to be that if any of the arbitrators have neglected either of the provisions, and the parties proceed with the arbitration and an award is made, the non-compliance would be an irregularity which would not invalidate the award; but if before actual award is made any of the parties becomes aware of the irregularity and takes the objection, he can refuse to attend, and an award made thereafter would probably be a nullity.

See Rennie vs. Utterson (unreported), decided by Mr. Justice Ferguson, 1893.

Gunn vs. Hallett, L.R. 14 Equity, p. 555.

10. Unless the contrary is agreed on, a submission to arbitration under this Act shall not be revoked or affected by the Submission not revoked death of any party thereto, but the by death of parties. matters in difference may be determined in the same manner as if the award had been made in his lifetime, subject to any rules of evidence relating to claims against the estates of deceased persons; and his executors or administrators shall be deemed to be a party to the submission.

This section was drawn to meet the general rule of law that in case of the death of a party the submission thereby was revoked, and the provision as to the rules of evidence is intended to safe guard the rights of his representatives under the ordinary law, which requires under the Evidence Act, R. S. O. (1887), Cap. 61, Sec. 10, that the evidence of a party who seeks any remedy against the estate shall not recover unless his evidence is corroborated by some other material evidence.

See also Radford vs. McDonald, 18 A. R p. 167.

The justice of this provision in the Statute is at once apparent, as it might happen that two parties were proceeding with an arbitration when one of them should die, and while the general law would protect his estate, as in case of his death the mere oath of the other party could not substantiate a claim against him without corroboration, yet under this Statute if he had signed a submission to arbitration his estate might be mulct in a large sum but for this provision, on the mere uncorroborated testimony of his opponent. The corroboration that is required is not corroboration in every essential, but that the evidence of the party shall be strengthened by evidence which appreciably helps the judicial mind to believe one or more of the material statements or facts deposed to.

It is not necessary that the case should be wholly proved by independent testimony.

11. Unless the submission contains words purporting that the parties intend that it shall not be made a rule or order of court, any party to the submission may at any time after the making of the *Submission may be made a rule of court.* award or certificate thereunder file such award or certificate together with the submission or a copy thereof (certified by the registrar aforesaid) in the office of the registrar of any of the divisions of the High Court of Justice.

12. The filing of an award or certificate together with the submission under the provisions of this Act shall have the same effect as the making of a submis- *Effect of filing award or certificate.* sion to arbitration a rule or order of said court has under the existing law and practice of said court ; and all provisions of the Act intituled *An Act respecting Arbitrations and References*, and of the amendments thereto, so far as the same relate to the enforcement of awards under voluntary submissions, shall be applicable to the enforcing of awards under this Act.

These sections are inserted so as to obtain the benefit of the provisions of the Arbitration Act, R.S.O. 1887, Cap. 53, Sections 13 and following, but the effect of those sections must be limited so as to harmonize with certain other provisions in the Act under discussion, and the latter part of the 12th section points more particularly to the obtaining of the benefit of section 45 of the Act, as many of the other provisions are modified by the provisions of this Act, notably the provisions relating to the enlargement of time, etc., and the provisions enabling the Court to revoke the submission or to set aside the award.

13. The Registrar, on the application of any party, by himself or his agent, may issue a summons for service by such party, commanding the attendance for Compelling attendance on arbitrations. examination of any witness, and also the production of any document, to and before the arbitrator or arbitrators, and at the time and place mentioned in the summons; and the disobedience of such summons shall render such witness liable to the same extent and in the same manner as the disobedience of a subpœna issued out of the High Court of Justice duly served, with an appointment of an arbitrator before whom the attendance is required under similar circumstances as now provided by law. Such summons may be to the effect of Form D in the schedule to this Act.

This is a most salutary provision, saving, as it does, the expense of issuing a subpœna in the High Court which would be necessary in ordinary arbitration under Sections 46 and 47 R. S O., Cap. 53, and gives the subpœna the same force and effect as a subpœna from the High Court of Justice.

A nice question may arise under the power to compel the production of documents, as under the 46th section of the Arbitration Act it is especially provided that no person shall be compelled to produce under a subpœna any writing or other documents that he would not be compelled to produce at a trial, whereas this section would apparently compel the production of any document, even if such production may tend in other proceedings to criminate the party, as this is within the jurisdiction of the Provincial Legislature.

The difficulty would, however, be obviated by the witness refusing to produce such a document, when the party seeking the production would be compelled to move as for contempt of Court, when the latter part of the section would probably be invoked and the Court would probably refuse to commit for contempt on such a case, as otherwise greater power would be vested in the Registrar than the Court itself can exercise

14. The arbitrator or arbitrators shall be at liberty to proceed in the absence of any party who, after reasonable notice neglects, or refuses to attend on the reference without having previously shewn to the arbitrator or arbitrators what such arbitrator or arbitrators shall consider good and sufficient cause for omitting to attend. *Arbitrators may proceed ex parte.*

This section avoids difficulties that have arisen where the party has refused to or neglected to attend Bass vs. Helsham, L.R. 2, Ex. 72.

15. Parties giving evidence before the arbitrator or arbitrators shall be examined on oath or affirmation, which may be administered by the arbitrators, or one of the arbitrators, or by the registrar. All parties shall produce before the arbitrator or arbitrators all documents within their possession or control which the arbitrator or arbitrators may require or call for. *Witnesses to be examined on oath. Production of documents.*

This section modifies the practice which prevailed under the Arbitration Act, as found in Section 48,

C

which allowed the parties to agree or consent to dispense with an oath or affirmation, and makes it incumbent upon the arbitrators in that case to administer an oath or affirmation. The latter part of the section would need to be read with Section 13 as to the production of documents, and gives very large powers indeed to the arbitrators.

Persons could be convicted of perjury before this tribunal in the same manner as if the evidence had been given in open court. Criminal Code (1892), Sec. 145.

Form of Oath.

A Christian is sworn on the New Testament. The arbitrator or umpire may repeat the following words : " The evidence which you shall give touching the matters in question shall be the truth, the whole truth, and nothing but the truth, so help you God." The witness holds the Testament in his right hand during the repetition of the form, and when the repetition is finished kisses the book. The above is the form of oath in common use ; a special form is, however, provided by schedule " C," (post, page) and it will perhaps be well to follow that form.

A Jew may be sworn on the Pentateuch with the same form of words as above, substituting the word " Jehovah " for " God."

A witness of any other religion may be sworn in such manner and with such ceremonies as he may declare to be binding on his conscience according to the religion he possesses. Omichund vs. Barker, (1 Sm. L.C.)

A Quaker, Menonist or Tunker, or a member of the

Moravian Church ("United Brethren") makes the following declaration, repeating it after the arbitrator : " I, A.B., do solemnly. sincerely and truly declare and affirm that I am one of the society called Quakers (or, as the case may be). I, A.B., do solemnly, sincerely and truly affirm and declare that the evidence which I shall give touching the matters in question shall be the truth, the whole truth, and nothing but the truth." R S.O., cap. 61, sec. 12.

A witness who refuses or is unwilling, from alleged conscientious motives, to be sworn, may be allowed to make the following declaration : " I, A.B., do solemnly, sincerely and truly affirm and declare that the taking of an oath is, according to my religious belief, unlawful ; and I do also solemnly, sincerely and truly affirm and declare that the evidence which I shall give touching the matters in question shall be the truth, the whole truth, and nothing but the truth." R.S.O., cap. 61, sec. 13.

A witness who objects to take an oath, or who is objected to as incompetent to take an oath, shall, if the arbitrator is satisfied that the taking of an oath would have no binding effect on his conscience, make the following promise, affirmation and declaration :

" I solemnly promise, affirm and declare that the evidence given by me shall be the truth, the whole truth, and nothing but the truth. —R. S. O., cap. 61, sec. 14.

Note.—The more extended wording provided by Schedule " C " of this Act may be used instead of the shorter expression suggested in the foregoing forms of declaration.

A person making any of the above declarations subjects himself to the same penalties as if he had been sworn in the ordinary way.—Dom. Stat, 56 Vict, cap. 31, sec. 24, s.s. 2.

16. The arbitrator or arbitrators shall make his or their award within twenty-one days after the signing of the submission, or on or before any later day to *Power to enlarge time for award.* which he or they may, in writing signed by him or them from time to time, enlarge the period for making the award.

This section would need to be strictly followed, as if by error or neglect the time was allowed to elapse without enlargement, it is not likely that the ordinary provision of the law would be applicable, viz. : that the Court may for cause enlarge the time, since the provisions of the Act respecting arbitrators, and reference under section 12, are only made applicable when the award and certificate together with submission are filed in the Court, and as this could not take place until the award is made, the parties would probably be held restricted to the rights given by this Statute.

17 The arbitrator or arbitrators shall make and publish his or their awards in writing, signed by the arbitrator or *Award to be in writing.* arbitrators making the same, and shall deposit the same with the registrar ; and every party to the reference may have a copy thereof upon payment of ten cents per folio of one hundred words, and the fees hereinafter provided for, unless already paid,

18. The hearing of every case shall, so far as circumstances permit, and subject to such adjournments as the arbitrator or arbitrators shall think necessary or just, be continued *de die in diem*.

Arbitrations to continue de die in diem.

The clear intention of the Legislation is a speedy hearing and conclusion of the case, and the arbitrators should not enlarge, except under such circumstances as a Judge would enlarge or postpone a case the trial of which had once commenced, and these of course vary according to the nature and circumstances of the case ; but speaking generally it should be shewn that some necessary and material witness is absent, whose attendance cannot be obtained at the particular time, or whose attendance reasonable diligence has been used to obtain, or that one of the parties has been taken by surprise by the nature of evidence adduced by the other, the evidence being such as he may not reasonably have expected to be given.

It must, however, always be left to the judical discretion of the arbitrators to decide whether an enlargment can fairly be given, always bearing in mind that a considerable onus is cast upon the party seeking it to show that the interests of justice require same.

In fixing an adjourned hearing, the hour at which the hearing will commence on the date fixed should be speci ed and a note thereof made by the arbitrators. If possible, a day should be fixed convenient to all parties, otherwise, when the day arrives an application will probably be made for a further adjournment, and there will be a needless waste of time and expense.

A party intending to apply for an adjournment on

the ground that he cannot attend a particular meeting, should give notice beforehand to the other parties of his intention to apply. This will give them an opportunity of saving the expense of bringing witnesses if they intend not to oppose the application. If a party does not do so it is likely that the arbitrators will under the power given them in Section 28, impose upon him or withhold from him all costs occasioned by his default.

19. If any party desires to be represented by a barrister, solicitor or agent, he shall, before the hearing, give two days' notice thereof to the registrar, and the **Barristers and Solicitors.** registrar shall forthwith communicate the information to the other party, who thereafter shall have the privilege of being represented by a barrister, solicitor or agent without any notice.

A party having either a barrister, solicitor or agent, the latter meaning any person appointed as such under the succeeding section, employs the same at his own expense, in all cases. No power is given to allow anything for the costs of such attendance.

20. Every person other than a barrister or solicitor appearing as the representative of any party shall file with the registrar a letter signed by such party **Authority of agents.** authorizing such person to appear for him; otherwise such person shall not, without the consent of the other party or parties, be allowed to take any part in the proceedings.

21. The attendance of parties may be dispensed with if they prefer jointly to state a case, file with the registrar, and agree to accept the decision of the arbitrators on such case. The award then shall be made on such stated case.

Special case.

In England, the arbitrators can if they desire, state a case for the opinion of the Court. The jurisdiction of the Court in such matters, submitted to it, is consultative and no appeal will lie from its decision. See Re Knight & Tabernacle Building Soc'y. W.N. 1892, p. 139.

But there is nothing in Ontario, authorizing the arbitrator to state a case for the opinion of the Court. The power in England is given by Sec. 19 of the Act of 1889, which reads: "Any referee, arbitrator or umpire, at any stage of the proceedings under a reference, shall, if so directed by the Court or a judge, state in the form of a special case for the opinion of the Court, any question of law arising in the course of the reference."

22. The sittings of arbitrators shall be considered private, and no person shall be admitted thereto during the hearing of a case except the parties, and their legal adviser or authorized agents and witnesses; provided always that any other persons may be present by permission of the arbitrators, unless objected to by any of the parties. Such permission shall not be granted to reporters of the public press without the special request of all parties interested in the case,

Sittings to be private.

23. The award may be set aside for fraud, but not for any other cause. Unless it is so set aside, the award shall be binding and conclusive upon the parties thereto, and be a final settlement of the matter in difference.

Award may be set aside for fraud.

This section is very important and is a complete revolution of the ordinary practice. What would be considered as fraud, would apparently be some personal misconduct in the arbitration, or a collusion between the arbitrator and one of the parties, or a corrupt bargain of any kind. It cannot be too strongly impressed upon arbitrators that they should not listen to suggestions from either side or give effect to anything that is not properly before them in evidence. Under the latter part of the section, which makes the award a final settlement of the matter in difference, great care should be taken in setting out clearly what is the matter which is agreed to be referred, and anything which was clearly contemplated by the parties when the agreement to refer was made, will be held to fall within this finality. See Turnock vs. Sartoris, 43 Ch.D. 150 (1890); Joplin vs. Postlethwaite, 61, L.T. 629 (1890); *Re* Carlisle, Clegg vs. Clegg, 44 C.D. 200 (1890); Wallis vs. Hirsch, 26 L.J. C.P. 72 (1856). And as subsidiary questions not fully contemplated by the parties, arise upon the hearing of an arbitration, it may be advisable to add in the written submission after the words, " All matters in difference between them in relation to the premises," etc., "or all matters in dispute in reference to," and the words, " Or any further matters of difference between the parties which may arise out of the above matters, during the hearing of this reference," or words to this effect. A form of reference containing such words will be found post, p. —, being "M2" of the forms given.

If it is intended to refer any question relating to the title to land or any pure question of law, it should be made sufficiently clear that these are intended to be referred, and if it is desired to give a power to decide as to an indemnity to be given by one party to another, against contingent claims, this should be stated. See Ross vs. Boards, 8 A. & E. 290 (1838).

Injunctions.

The High Court has a power to restrain by injunction the proceedings in an arbitration where the arbitrator is, for any special reason, unfit or incompetent to act. Such grounds of incompetence would be : Personal interest ; that he has been convicted of perjury or fraud ; or, when in the absence of a conviction, he would be obviously unfit for the exercise of judicial functions. See Jessel M.R. in Beddow vs. Beddow, 9 Ch.D. 89 (1878), and Malmesbury Railway Co. vs. Budd 2 Ch.D 113 (1876).

It is, however, clear that the Court will not interfere by injunction merely because an arbitrator is exceeding his jurisdiction, or because the proceedings are futile and oppressive. N. London Ry. Co. vs. G. N. Ry. Co , 11 Q B.D. 30 (1883), and London and Blackwall Ry. Co. vs Cross, 31 Ch.D. 354 (1886). In the later case of Farrar vs. Cooper, 44 Ch.D. 323 (1890), there is a dictum of Kekewitch, J., to the effect that there may be cases in which the Court will interfere by injunction, on the ground that injustice or injury would result to the party complaining.

24. Any motion to set aside the award for fraud must be made within one month after the discovery of such fraud.

25. A commission to take the testimony of any person without the Province, or of any aged or infirm person resident within the Province, or of a person who is about to withdraw therefrom, may be allowed by the arbitrator or arbitrators and may issue in the same manner and with the same effect as in an action brought in the High Court of Justice.

The practice in this is regulated by the Judicature Act, and all that would seem to be necessary to found the application would be the production of the ruling of the arbitrator, shewing that a matter was proceeding before him under this Act, and that in the opinion of the arbitrator or arbitrators a commission was necessary, when an order would no doubt be at once granted by the Master in Chambers, and upon the return of the commission, the evidence would be receivable as in ordinary cases in the High Court of Justice.

26. In any case not provided for by this Act, the law and practice relating to voluntary submissions to arbitration shall be applicable.

This section is a most important one, as where the Act does not specially provide, the parties are not left

without remedy, but may invoke the provisions of the
Arbitration Act. An instance of where the two
might clash would be the combined effect of sections
12 and 16 before adverted to.

27. Five days' clear notice at least of the
time fixed for the hearing of any case
shall be given by the registrar to all Notice of
hearing.
parties to the submission, unless all
parties otherwise agree.

28. The costs of the reference and award shall
be in the discretion of the arbitrator or
arbitrators, who shall have power to Costs in discretion of
arbitrator.
direct to and by whom and in what
manner and within what time the same shall be
paid. No fees or costs shall be payable except
witness' fees, arbitrators' fees, registrar's fees, and
office fees.

(2) A witness shall be entitled to the same
fees as in an action in the High Court of Justice.

The schedule of fees under this would be as follows :—

To ordinary witnesses residing within three
    miles of the place where the arbitration is
    being held, per diem $1 00
To ordinary witnesses residing more than three
    miles from such place, per diem..........$1 25
Barristers and solicitors, physicians and surgeons
    other than parties to the reference, when call-
    ed upon to give evidence in consequence of
    any professional services rendered by them, or
    to give professional opinions, per diem......$4 00

Engineers and architects, not parties to the reference, when called upon to give evidence
of professional service rendered by them, or to
give evidence depending upon their skill or
judgment, per diem.....................$4 00
An auctioneer was held entitled to professional
fees in *Re* Workingmen's Mutual Society, 21
Ch. D. 831.
Surveyors (under the Surveyors' Act, R. S. O.,
Cap. 152, sec. 25 (5)) per diem $5 00

Witnesses residing more than three miles from the
place where the arbitration is held are entitled to
their travelling expenses, reasonably and actually
paid, but in no case exceeding 20 cents per mile one
way.

The costs of witnesses called to prove irrelevant
matters should not be allowed :—Christopher vs.
Noxon, 10 P. R., 149.

If a witness is subpœnaed but not called, the arbitrators may enquire into the practicability and necessity of subpœnaing him : McLean vs. Evans, 3 P.R.
154. The expenses of such witnesses were not allowed in a case where the evidence expected from them
was apparently of no value, and they were summoned
from abundance of caution :—Beddington vs. Deich-
mann, 80 L. T. Jour. 226.

When the plaintiff was a necessary and material
witness in his own behalf, and came from England to
give evidence, his travellihg expenses were allowed :

> Fox vs Toronto and Nipissing Railway Co., 7
> P.R. 157 ; Talbot vs. Poole, 15 P.R. 274
> (1893).

The amount to be allowed for procuring the attendance of witnesses who live out of Ontario is apparently in the discretion of the arbitrator, and is not limited to the amounts above specified :   See Ball vs. Crompton Corset Co., 11 P.R. 256, where an expert brought from Buffalo to give evidence was allowed $33.00 per day and expenses.

29. The fees for arbitration under this Act shall be as follows : For each arbitrator who shall be present at the hearing of any case, a fee of not more than $5 for *Arbitrators' fees* each sitting ; office fee, including registrar's assistance, forms, rooms, etc., $5 for the first sitting, and $3 for each sitting thereafter, the arbitrator or arbitrators to apportion such sum out of this as they see fit to the registrar for his attendance. The above scale shall apply unless the parties enter into an agreement in writing to pay specified fees of a larger amount.

In cases of an important nature the parties will probably find it to their interest to agree upon a fixed rate for the arbitrators, either by way of a per diem allowance or lump sum, which agreement should be in writing and filed with the Registrar, and upon its being entered into, the scale therein agreed to shall govern.

All the arbitrators should attend during the whole hearing, otherwise the award may be avoided, each arbitrator having an individual duty to hear and decide upon the evidence.   See Creswell J. in Beck vs. Jackson 1 C.B., N.S. 695 (1857).

If three arbitrators are appointed and one neglects

to attend, two who attend during the whole hearing can give a valid award. See Young vs. Bulman, 13 C.B., 623.

30. The award of the majority of the arbitrators shall be as binding and conclusive as the award of all three without any provision to that effect in the agreement; and any act which is directed by this Act to be done by a board of arbitrators shall be valid if done by any two of them; and in case of the appointment of three arbitrators the neglect or refusal of any arbitrator to act shall not invalidate the proceedings, but all proceedings may be taken by the majority of the board appointed under this Act.

Award of majority to be binding.

31. In case both parties to the submission refuse or neglect to take up the award within three days after notice has been sent by the registrar to the said parties by mail at their last known place of business or residence, then the registrar shall be entitled to obtain an order from the arbitrators or a majority of them for the payment of the fees hereinbefore provided for; and upon such order being produced to the clerk of the county court of the county he shall file the same, and shall issue execution in the name of the registrar against the goods and lands of the party or parties named therein as upon a judgment in such court, for the amount of such fees, and the costs proper to be taxed in the discretion of such clerk for the order and execution; and such execution shall have the same force and effect as an execution in any case in the said court.

Recovery of fees where award not taken up

This section is of great importance to the arbitrators and the registrar, as very often parties neglect to take up an award, and the arbitrators are put to a great deal of expense in order to collect their fees.

32. The Council of the Board of Trade may make any rules and regulations for the efficient carrying out of the objects of this Act and the awards made thereunder, provided that the same are not inconsistent with the provisions of this Act
Board may make rules.

33. This Act is not intended in any way to interfere or qualify the provisions of the Act relating to the Board of Trade of the City of Toronto, or to arbitrations between the members thereof, or to the by-laws and rules framed under such Act.
This Act not to affect arbitrations between members of the board.

In the case of arbitrations between members of the Board of Trade it will be well if they are intended to be brought under this Act that it should be expressly so stated in the agreement or submission, otherwise the arbitration will be of a very different character to that outlined in this Act.

34, Upon the application of a Board of Trade duly formed in pursuance of the Revised Statute of Canada, chapter 130, respecting the incorporation of Boards of Trade, or otherwise, in any city of this Province having at least 30,000 inhabitants according to the last preceding Dominion or municipal census, the Lieutenant-Governor in
Formation of boards of arbitration in other cities.

Council may direct that such Board of Trade of such city may avail itself of the provisions of this Act and form a chamber of Arbitration as provided by this Act in the case of the Board of Trade of the City of Toronto, and such Board of Trade so availing itself of this Act shall, after the Order-in-Council, have all the powers conferred by this Act upon the Board of Trade of the City of Toronto.

(2) The Order-in-Council shall be sufficient evidence that the city named therein is a city to which this section is applicable.

(3) A copy of the Order-in-Council shall be laid before the Legislative Assembly at the first session after the making of such Order.

SCHEDULE A.

(Section 7.)

Agreement made this   day of   1894, between   of   and   of

Whereas differences have arisen between the parties hereto in respect of   and they have agreed to refer such differences to arbitration upon the terms and conditions contained in the Act of the Legislature of the Province of Ontario intituled *An Act enabling Boards of Trade in Cities to appoint general arbitrators for certain purposes* :

Now it is hereby agreed by the said parties that all matters in difference between them in relation to the premises shall be and are hereby referred to

and   and,

in case they cannot agree upon a third arbitrator within three days, to such third arbitrator as the registrar of the chamber of arbitrators may select.

In witness whereof the said parties have hereunto set their hands and seals.

Signed, sealed and delivered⎫
    in the presence of ⎭

SCHEDULE B.

(Section 9.)

FORM OF OATHS BY ARBITRATORS.

I, solemnly swear that I will faithfully, diligently and impartially perform my duty as arbitrator, and I will, (in all cases) (*or* in the case between and now) submitted to me, give a true and just award according to the best of my judgment and ability, without fear, favor, affection of or for any party or person whomsoever. So help me God.

SCHEDULE C.

(Section 15.)

FORM OF OATH, WITNESSES.

You solemnly swear that you will true answer make to all such questions as shall be asked of you as a witness under examination in this case between
and
and therein, and you will to the best of your knowledge, information and belief, speak the truth, the whole truth and nothing but the truth. So help you God.

D

SCHEDULE D.

(Section 13.)

SUMMONS TO WITNESS.

In the matter of an arbitration between
A. B. and *C. D.*

Under the Boards of Trade General Arbitrations Act, 1894.

To *E. F.*

Whereas an arbitration between the above parties
is now pending ; and whereas
one of the parties thereto, desires that you should
attend before the arbitrator (*or* arbitrators) to give
evidence, and has (*or* have) authorized and required
me   as registrar to issue this summons for
your attendance, I do hereby in the exercise of the
powers in this behalf given by the said Act, summon
and require you to attend at   on   the
day of   at the hour of   in the   noon
of the said day at   before the said arbitrator
(*or* arbitrators) there to be examined and give evidence
dence on behalf of   and also to bring with
you and produce at the time and place aforesaid
(*specify documents to be produced*).

In default of your attending at the time and place
aforesaid, you are liable to be proceeded against
under the provisions of *The Boards of Trade General Arbitrations Act, 1894.*

In witness whereof I have hereto set my hand this
day of

PART II.

APPENDIX A.

RULES AND FORMS

OF THE

Toronto Chamber of Arbitration

RULES.

NAME.

1. This Institution shall be called the Toronto Chamber of Arbitration.

OFFICES.

2. The Offices of the Chamber shall be in the Board of Trade Building, in the City of Toronto, Province of Ontario.

OBJECT.

3. The Chamber shall be available both for voluntary references to Arbitration and for the Arbitration of cases referred to it by the Courts of Law and the Judges thereof.

NOMINATION AND ELECTION OF ARBITRATORS.

4. It shall be the duty of the Council of the Board of Trade of the City of Toronto to nominate from the community generally not less than thirty persons, out of which number there shall be

elected by ballot by the members of the Board, at a special meeting called for that purpose, twenty-five persons, who shall form the Toronto Chamber of Arbitration.

CONSENT OF ARBITRATORS TO ACT.

5. It shall be the duty of the Council of the Board of Trade of the City of Toronto to obtain the written consent of each person nominated, in the Form A. in the Appendix, before presenting same to the General Board. Immediately after the election of the required number of Arbitrators, a list of the persons elected shall be published in the " Ontario Gazette," and the names of the members of the Board of Arbitrators shall be continuously posted in the offices of the Board in the Board of Trade Building.

APPROVAL OF ARBITRATORS BY THE GENERAL BOARD.

6. Upon the election by the General Board of the necessary number of Arbitrators, it shall be the duty of the Registrar to forthwith send a notice in the Form marked B. in the Appendix, to each person appointed.

QUALIFICATIONS OF ARBITRATORS.

7. Persons qualified for appointment as Arbitrators shall be British subjects, and all such other persons as in the opinion of the Council of the Board of Trade shall be specially qualified. If convicted of any indictable offence his appoint-

ment to act as such Arbitrator shall thereby
forthwith be vacated.

8. The Chamber shall provide the parties who submit to Arbitration under its Rules with Arbitration rooms and all necessary forms and papers,
and shall do or cause to be done all such acts as
it lawfully may do for the purpose of assisting
the parties and the Arbitrators in the course of
an Arbitration.

NUMBER AND SELECTION OF ARBITRATORS.

9. All Arbitrations under these Rules shall be held
before one, two, or three Arbitrators, according
to the desire of the parties. The Arbitrator or
Arbitrators shall be selected from the approved
list by the Registrar of the Chamber, according
to the nature of the dispute; unless the parties
have previously agreed upon an Arbitrator or
Arbitrators selected from such list.

(*b*) If the Reference be to two Arbitrators they
shall, before entering on the Reference, appoint
a third Arbitrator (form J.) to be selected by
them from the approved list, and if they fail to
appoint such third Arbitrator within three days
from the appointment of the last appointed of
them, the Registrar shall, upon the application
(form K.) of either of them, or of any party to
the Reference, forthwith appoint a third Arbitrator from such list, who shall have the like
power to act in the Reference and make an
award as if he had been appointed by consent of
all parties.

10. The Registrar shall in every case send to each
selected Arbitrator a notice of his selection.
Such notice shall be in one of the forms marked
C. or E. in the Appendix hereto, according to
the nature of the case. Every such notice shall
be accompanied by a declaration in one of the
forms marked D. F. or H. in the Appendix,
which the Arbitrator shall sign and return to
the Registrar. If the appointment of the Arbitrator or Arbitrators rests with the Registrar,
the Registrar shall, upon receipt of such declaration notifying that the Arbitrator or Arbitrators assents or assent to act in the particular
case for which he or they have been selected,
send to the Arbitrator or Arbitrators notice of
his or their appointment which shall be in the
Form marked I. in the Appendix.

In any case where after submission, but before
award, the Reference is determined by the act of
the parties, then if the same is so determined
before notice has been given to the Registrar by
the selected Arbitrator or Arbitrators of his or
their assent to act in the particular case, the
Arbitrator or Arbitrators shall not be entitled to
any fees ; but if it is so determined after such
notice has been given, then there shall forthwith
be paid to the Registrar for the selected Arbitrator or Arbitrators, by the several parties to
the submission, in equal shares, the specified fees
for such time as the Arbitrator or Arbitrators

shall have sat to hear the case, and if he or they
shall not at the time of such determination have
sat to hear the case, then such fees as he or they
would have been entitled to if he or they had
held a sitting for that purpose.

No provision appears to be made as to how the
notices mentioned are to be served by the Registrar
or a party as the case may be, but it would seem
clear that "giving notice" means giving notice in the
ordinary course of post. The whole object of the Act
and rules is to enable the parties to get to work without
delay caused by any wilful neglect, or inattention by
a party or an arbitrator, and the rule would be un-
workable if, say in the case of an arbitrator who had
failed to act by going abroad, a party had to show
that the notice calling upon him to act had reached
him personally.

*Under Rules 9 and 10 the application to the Regis-
trar can be made ex parte.   In appointing a third arbitrator, arbitrators are exercising a judicial duty and
must use their judgment in the selection.   In Pescod
vs. Pescod, 58 L. T. 76 (1888), an appointment made
under the following circumstances was set aside by the
Court.   The arbitrators were unable to decide between
two persons, each wrote the name of his nominee on a
slip of paper.   The slips were placed in a hat and the
waiter was called in to draw the lot.   The person whose
name was drawn was appointed by the arbitrators.
Nevertheless if both of the disputants have agreed to
or acquiesced in the arbitrators taking such a course,
the award will not be set aside on the ground that the*

umpire was improperly appointed.   *Re Tunno & Bird,*
5 B. & Ad. 488 (1823).

HOLIDAYS.

11. The offices of the Chamber shall be closed, and
no Arbitrations shall be held under these Rules
on Sundays and public holidays.

OFFICERS OF THE CHAMBER.

12. The officers of the Chamber shall be the Secretary
of the Board of Trade of the City of Toronto
(unless the Council of the Board make a separate appointment,) and such other officers as the
Council shall from time to time determine who
shall hold office during the pleasure of the
Council.

DUTIES OF REGISTRAR.

13. The Secretary of the Board shall be Registrar.
     The duties of the Registrar shall be as fol-
lows : He shall by himself or his subordinate receive submissions and payment of fees and costs,
select and notify Arbitrators, give notice of hearing to parties, keep a Register of Submissions,
a Register of Awards and Reconciliations, and
such other books and memoranda, and make such
returns as the Council of the Board of Trade of
the City of Toronto shall from time to time require. He shall render such assistance to the
Arbitrator or Arbitrators in an Arbitration as
he or they may require, and generally carry out
the instructions of the Council.

DEPUTY-REGISTRAR.

The Deputy-Registrar, appointed by the Council of the Board of Trade of the City of Toronto, shall, during the Registrar's absence, perform the duties of Registrar, and at other times shall discharge such duties as the Registrar may direct.

FORMS OF SUBMISSION TO BE SIGNED.

14. If two or more persons have a difference which they wish determined by Arbitration, under the rules of the Toronto Chamber of Arbitration, they shall fill up and sign one of the forms of submission mentioned in and set out in the appendix hereto.—Form M.

ARBITRATIONS IN PURSUANCE OF SUBMISSION IN CONTRACTS.

15. Whenever a written contract contains a submission of any disputes which may arise, relating to such contract to Arbitration, under the rules of the Toronto Chamber of Arbitration, without further specifying any particular mode of Arbitration under such rules, such disputes shall (subject as hereinafter provided), upon the written application of any party to such submission, addressed to the Registrar, be submitted to the Arbitration of an Arbitrator selected by the Registrar, and it shall not be necessary for the parties to sign any further submission, but all the terms and provisions contained in the form of submission to an Arbitrator, to be selected by

the Registrar, which may for the time being be
prescribed by the Chamber, shall have the same
force and effect, and be binding upon the parties
in the same manner as though such terms and
provisions had been fully set out and expressed
in the submission contained in the said contract,
save that the time within which an award shall
be made in such Arbitration shall begin to run
only from the date on which the Registrar shall
notify the selection of the Arbitrator to the parties.   Provided, nevertheless, that if the parties
to the said submission so agree, they may, notwithstanding any thing in this rule b fore contained, upon dispute arising, sign any form of
submission, for the time being prescribed by the
Chamber, and appoint or procure to be appointed an Arbitrator or Arbitrators thereunder, in which case the dispute shall be determined in accordance with the terms and provisions of the submission so signed.

ARBITRATIONS IN PURSUANCE OF AN ORDER OF COURT.

16. Whenever in any proceeding in a Court of Law
or Equity, matters in difference between the
parties to such proceeding are by the Order of
the Court referred to Arbitration, and, by consent of the parties, such Order directs that said
matters in difference, be referred to Arbitration
under the Rules of the Toronto Chamber of Arbitration, or to that effect, without specifying
any particular mode of Arbitration under such
Rules, the said matters in difference shall (sub-

ject as hereinafter provided), upon the written application of any party to such Order, addressed to the Registrar, be submitted to the Arbitration of an Arbitrator selected by the Registrar, and it shall not be necessary for the parties to such Order, to sign any further submission, but all the terms and provisions contained in the form of submission to an Arbitrator, to be selected by the Registrar, which may for the time being be prescribed by the Chamber, shall have the same force and effect, and be binding upon the said parties, in the same manner as though such terms and provisions had been fully set out and expressed in the said Order, save that the time within which an award shall be made in such Arbitration shall begin to run only from the date on which the Registrar shall notify the selection of the Arbitrators to the parties. Provided, nevertheless, that if the parties to the said Order so agree, they may, notwithstanding anything in this Rule before contained, sign any form of submission for the time being prescribed by the Chamber, and appoint or procure to be appointed, an Arbitrator or Arbitrators thereunder, in which case the said matters in difference shall be determined in accordance with the terms and provisions of the submission so signed.

FAILURE OF ARBITRATORS TO ACT.

17. (a) If before award a sole Arbitrator or one of three Arbitrators dies or becomes incapable of acting, or declines to act, or seven days after

notice from the parties or any of them, or from the Registrar, fails to act, the parties may, or if such Arbitrator was appointed by the Registrar, the Registrar, on application by any of the parties, may appoint a new Arbitrator to act in his stead, and if such Arbitrator was appointed by the parties, and the parties fail to appoint a new Arbitrator, any party may serve the other party, or parties, with a written notice to agree upon the appointment of a new Arbitrator, and if such appointment is not made within four days after the service of such notice, the Registrar may, on the application of the party who gave such notice, appoint a new Arbitrator.

(b) Any Arbitrator appointed by the Registrar under this rule shall be selected from the approved list, and shall have like powers to act in the Reference, and to make an award as if he had been appointed by consent of all parties.

NO ACTION TO BE BROUGHT.

18. No party to a submission shall bring any action, or commence, or prosecute any proceeding, either at law or in equity, against an Arbitrator or any other party to the submission concerning the matters referred, or any of them.

EXTENSION OF TIME FOR GIVING NOTICES.

19. In case any party to a reference resides outside the City of Toronto, the Registrar may, at his discretion, enlarge the time for the performance by such party of any act required or authorized to be done by these rules.

RECONCILIATIONS.

20. If after signing the submission, all parties shall have reconciled their difference before the case comes on for hearing, the parties may sign an agreement in the form marked L. in the Appendix hereto, and the same shall be entered in a Register kept for that purpose by the Chamber, and copies thereof shall be delivered by the Re· gistrar to any of the parties thereto upon payment of the fees specified in the Act.

LEGAL ASSESSORS.

21. (a) There shall be a legal assessor to the said Chamber of Arbitration, who shall, unless otherwise appointed by the Council of the Board of Trade, be the Solicitor for the Board of Trade, and in case of his absence or inability to attend, then he shall nominate his representative who shall act as such assessor, and such assessors shall hold office during the pleasure of the Council of the Board of Trade.

(b) The arbitrator or arbitrators or any two of them may request (form N.) the attendance of such assessor to advise and assist him or them in the arbitration, and he shall be entitled, if so desired, to sit with the arbitrator or arbitrators, who may submit any question to him for his determination and their guidance.

(c) The parties may, if they so desire, also request the attendance of such assessor, such request being signified by the parties to the Registrar (form O.) in writing, and thereupon the assessor shall sit with the arbitrator or arbitrators for the purpose of advising or assisting him or them in the arbitration.

(*d*) Neither such assessor, nor any member of any legal firm with which he may be connected, shall take part on behalf of any parties, in any arbitration under these rules.

(*e*) Such arbitrator or arbitrators may pay a reasonable fee, to be fixed by him or them, unless the parties agree upon the amount, to such assessor for any such attendance or advice which shall be added to the said arbitrator or arbitrators' fees, and form part of the costs of arbitration as such.

FORM OF SUBMISSION.

22. The form of submission to arbitration shall be in the form M., to these rules.

TIME.

23. In any case in which any particular number of days, not expressed to be clear days, is prescribed by these Rules, the same shall be reckoned exclusively of the first day and inclusively of the last day.

Where any limited time less than six days, from or after any date or event, is appointed or allowed for doing any act, or taking any proceeding, Sundays or public holidays shall not be reckoned in the computation of such limited time.

Where the time for doing any act, or taking

any proceedings, expires on a Sunday, or other day on which the offices of the Chamber are closed, such act or proceeding shall, so far as regards the time of doing or taking the same, be considered to be duly done, or taken if done or taken on the day on which the offices shall next be open.

ALTERATIONS OF RULES.

24. The Council of the Board of Trade of the City of Toronto may from time to time alter, amend, add to, or omit any of these Rules as may be found expedient, opportunity being previously afforded to the Board of Trade of the City of Toronto to submit suggestions with regard to any proposed alterations, and to be heard thereon.

FORMS.

A.

Form of Assent to Nomination as Arbitrator.

TORONTO CHAMBER OF ARBITRATION.

It having been intimated to me by
that it is desired to nominate me as an
Arbitrator of the Toronto Chamber of Arbitration,
I hereby express my willingness to act, subject to the
Rules of the said Chamber for the time being in force.

(Signed)

Postal Address.

Date,

B.

THE BOARD OF TRADE OF THE CITY OF TORONTO.

Secretary's Office,

Toronto,   189   .

TORONTO CHAMBER OF ARBITRATION.

Form of Appointment as Arbitrator.

The Board of Trade of the City of Toronto doth
hereby appoint   to act as an
Arbitrator of the Toronto Chamber of Arbitration,
subject to the Rules of the said Chamber for the time
being in force.

(Signed)

Registrar.

(64)

C.

Form of Notification of Appointment of Arbitrator by the Parties.

TORONTO CHAMBER OF ARBITRATION.

To

SIR,—

You have been appointed to act as *
Arbitrator to decide certain matters in difference
between   and
by a submission signed by them, and dated the
day of
You are requested to sign the accompanying form
declaring whether you assent or decline to act in the
above matter, and to return the same at your earliest
convenience to

Registrar.

Dated,

* Sole, or one of two, or one of three.

D.

Form of Declaration of Arbitrator Appointed by the Parties, Assenting or Declining to Act.

TORONTC CHAMBER OF ARBITRATION.

To the Registrar of the Toronto Chamber of Arbitration.

In the matter of a submission to Arbitration,

E

subject to the Rules of the Toronto Chamber of
Arbitration, between
and   dated the
day of   I hereby *
to act as an Arbitrator in the above Reference.

(Signed)

Dated,

* Assent or decline.

E.

Form of Notification of Appointment of Third Arbitrator by Two Arbitrators.

TORONTO CHAMBER OF ARBITRATION.

To

Sir, — You have been appointed by the Arbitrators
to act as third Arbitrator with regard to certain matters in difference between
and   which have been referred
to the said Arbitrators by a submission signed by the
said parties and dated the   day
of
You are requested to fill up and sign the accompanying form declaring whether you assent or decline
to act in the above matter, and to return the same
at your earliest convenience to

Registrar.

Dated,

F.

Form of Declaration of Third Arbitrator Appointed by Arbitrators, Assenting or Declining to Act.

TORONTO CHAMBER OF ARBITRATION.

To the Registrar of the Toronto Chamber of Arbitration.

In the matter of a submission to Arbitration, subject to the Rules of the Toronto Chamber of Arbitration, between
and   dated
the   day of
I hereby *   to act as third Arbitrator
in the above Reference.

                    (Signed)
Dated,
            * Assent or decline.

H.

Declaration in answer to request of Registrar to act as Arbitrator.

TORONTO CHAMBER OF ARBITRATION.

To the Registrar of the Toronto Chamber of Arbitration.

In the matter of a submission to Arbitration, subject to the rules of the Toronto Chamber of Arbitration, between

and   dated
the   day of
I hereby *   to act as X
in the above reference.

                (Signed)
Dated,
                *Assent or decline.

X, Sole Arbitrator, or one of two Arbitrators, or
one of three Arbitrators.

I.

Form of Appointment by Registrar of Arbitrator or Arbitrators.

TORONTO CHAMBER OF ARBITRATION.

To

In the matter of a submission to Arbitration
between   and
dated the   day of
you are hereby appointed, subject to the Rules of the
Toronto Chamber of Arbitration, to act as *
in the above reference.

                (Signed)
                            Registrar.
Dated, '

* Sole Arbitrator, or one of two Arbitrators, or one
  of three Arbitrators

J.

Appointment of third Arbitrator by two Arbitrators.

TORONTO CHAMBER OF ARBITRATION.

To

(Insert name of third Arbitrator appointed.)

In the matter of a submission to Arbitration, subject to the Rules of the Toronto Chamber of Arbitration, between

and   Dated

the   day of   , 18 .

We   of

and   of (the Arbitrators appointed by the above submission) hereby appoint you to act as third Arbitrator in this Reference, pursuant to Rule

(Signed)

of

of

Dated,

Both Arbitrators should sign this form at the same time, and should file the same with the Registrar.

K.

Application to the Registrar to appoint a third Arbitrator.

TORONTO CHAMBER OF ARBITRATION.

To the Registrar of the Toronto Chamber of Arbitration.

In the matter of a submission to Arbitration, subject to the Rules of the Toronto Chamber of Arbitra-

tion, between
and   Dated
the   day of   18   .

Whereas the Arbitrators appointed to act in this
Reference have failed to appoint a third Arbitrator
within ten days of their appointment, or the appointment of the last appointed of them. I hereby make
application to you to appoint a third Arbitrator
pursuant to Rule

(Signed)
of

(A party to the above submission (or) an
Arbitrator appointed in the above
submission).

--- ---

L.

Notice of Reconciliation.

TORONTO CHAMBER OF ARBITRATION.

Whereas by a submission to Arbitration, dated
the   day of   18   ,
we, the undersigned referred certain matters in difference between us to be determined by Arbitration.
And whereas we have settled all the said matters in
difference, we do hereby withdraw the said case from
Arbitration.

And we desire that the terms of our agreement be
entered in the Register of the Chamber. They are
as follows :—

Dated this   day of   18   .

(Signed)

M.

Form of Submission.

Agreement made this   day of
1894, between   of   and
          of
Whereas differences have arisen between the parties hereto in respect of   and
they have agreed to refer such differences to arbitration upon the terms and conditions contained in the
Act of the Legislature of the Province of Ontario intituled   " An Act enabling Boards of Trade in cities
to appoint general arbitrators for certain purposes."

Now it is Hereby Agreed by the said parties that
all matters in difference between them in relation to
the premises shall be and are hereby referred to
          and   and in
case they cannot agree upon a third arbitrator within
three days, to such third arbitrator as the Registrar
of the Chamber of Arbitration may select.   It is
agreed that the parties shall be governed by all the
rules of the Toronto Chamber of Arbitration which
are hereby made part of this bond as if specifically
written therein.

In witness Whereof the said parties have hereunto
set their hands and seals.

Signed, sealed and delivered ⎫
in the presence of ⎭

Form of submission suggested.   Ante p. 41.

M2.

Form of Submission.

Agreement made this   day of   189 ,
between   of   and
                  of
Whereas differences have arisen between the
parties hereto in respect of   and
they have agreed to refer such differences to arbitration upon the terms and conditions contained in the
Act of the Legislature of the Province of Ontario
intituled " An Act enabling Boards of Trade in
cities to appoint general arbitrators for certain
purposes."

Now it is Hereby Agreed by the said parties that
all matters in difference between them in relation
to premises or any further matters of difference between them which may arise out of the said matters
during the hearing of this reference shall be and are
hereby referred to   and
and in case they cannot agree upon a third arbitrator within three days, to such third arbitrator as the
Registrar of the Chamber of Arbitration may select.
It is agreed that the parties shall be governed by all
the rules of the Toronto Chamber of Arbitration
which are hereby made part of this bond as if
specifically written herein.

In witness whereof the said parties have hereunto
set their hands and seals.

Signed, sealed and delivered }
in the presence of   }

N.

Request for Attendance of Legal Assessor.

TORONTO CHAMBER OF ARBITRATION.

In the matter of a Submission to Arbitration, subject to the rules of the Toronto Chamber of Arbitration, between   and
dated the   day of   18   ; we, the   X
appointed to act in this reference desire the attendance of the Legal Assessor at the said Arbitration, subject to the rules of the Chamber.

Dated this   day of
(Signed)
To the Registrar.

X Arbitrator or Arbitrators.

O.

Request for Attendance of Legal Assessor.

TORONTO CHAMBER OF ARBITRATION.

Whereas by Submission to Arbitration, dated the
day of   ; we,
the undersigned, referred certain matters in difference between us to be determined by Arbitration ; we hereby give notice that we desire the attendance of the Legal Assessor at the said Arbitration, subject to the rules of the Chamber.

Dated this   day of
(Signed)
To the Registrar.

APPENDIX B.

TIME TABLE.

Term of office of Arbitrators (see p. 25) - 2 years.

Time for making award from date of submission, unless enlarged (see p. 36) - 21 days.

Notice by party to Registrar of intention to be represented by Barrister, Solicitor, or Agent (see p. 38) - - - - 2 days.

Time for motion to set aside for fraud (see p. 42) - - - - - - 1 month.

Notice of hearing given by Registrar to parties (see p. 43) - - - - 5 days.

Notice to Arbitrator requiring him to act (see p. 59) - - - - - - 7 days.

Notice to party or parties to appoint new Arbitrator (see p. 60) - - - 4 days.

The question of the calculation of time is dealt with by Rule 23 (see p. 62).

INDEX.

—◦✥◦—

	PAGE
Absence of Party	3
Actions against arbitrator	13, 60
against party to arbitration	60
agreement to refer no defence to an	9
Adjournments	37
costs of	38
Affirmation instead of oath	33, 35
form of	34, 35
Agent of party cannot be arbitrator	10
his authority to refer disputes	7
presence of	2
representation by	38
authority of	38
legal assessor not to act as	62
Alteration of rules	63
Amendment of rules	63
Application to Registrar may be ex-parte	55
for appointment of third arbitrator, form of	69
Arbitration, see Submission, Arbitration, Award	
what is	6, 7
in pursuance of a contract	57
in pursuance of order of court	58
proceedings before	13
parties to	7
matters to be referred to	8
between members of Board of Trade	47
boards of	23
names of members of to be published and posted up	25
who may attend	39
Arbitrator, action against	13, 60
agent of party can not be	10
and valuator compared	6
appointment of	23, 25, 51
by Registrar, form of	68
is for two years	25

PAGE

Arbitrator, appointment of, new...... 60
new by Registrar, form of........ 64
by parties, notification of 65
assent to act as, Form of........... 64
cannot state cause for opinion of court........... 39
consent of, to act 24, 52
death of 7, 39
discretion of, as to adjournment 37
witness fees................. .....44, 45
disqualification of, by crime.................... 25
dissenting, duty of......... 21
election of, to be notified ....• 51, 54
excess of Jurisdiction of 41
expert, as 24
failure of to act 59
fees of 45
included in costs................... 43
where reference not concluded........... 54
fixes order of business.....................14, 17
has discretion as to costs..................... 43
how chosen where reference by order of court..... 59
incompetency of 25, 41
manager of Company, as 10
may allow certain persons to attend............. 39
may decide as to contribution.... 7
may lump claims............ 19
may proceed ex-parte, when.................. 23
may request assessor to attend.... 61
may state special case.......................... 38
must act on legal evidence.................... 40
must decide all questions submitted............. 18
must hear both sides.......................... 14
must himself perform all judicial acts........... 14
must sign declaration 54
must not hear evidence ex-parte................ 14
must not reserve points for future determination.. 20
need not be member of Board of Trade........... 25
need not state reasons......................... 25
nomination of............................24, 51
notes of...................................... 17
oath of...................................... 49

                                                                PAGE
Arbitrator, objection to, how taken... 11
        performs judicial functions...................... 6
        refusal of, to attend............................ 46
        to be notified of appointment..... ....27, 56
        who dissents, duty of 21
        who may act as........ ....9, 52
        third, appointment of 53, 55, 56
Arbitrators, all, to attend whole hearing........ 46
        all to sign award at same time................21, 22
        award of two..... ....2, 46
        fees of.............................. 45
                where reference not concluded........... 54
                where award not taken up............... 46
        how chosen........................... 2
        list of, to be published and posted up 25, 52
        number of,....................................27, 53
        selection of, from list.......................53, 56
        to sign award 36
Attendance of parties...... ....3, 39
Attendance of witness how procured 32
Award, general requisites................................. 17
        attestation of 21
        binding if of majority of arbitrators. 45
        copy of, party may have 36
        costs, part of... 20
        description in, to be clear........ 22
        form of............................ ....20, 21
        filing, effect of................................. 40
        how enforced 4
        as to land conveyance............................ 20
        may be filed in High Court......... 31
                on case stated............................. 39
                set aside for fraud.......... 40
        motion to set aside 42
        must be certain........., ... 17
        must be final 18, 40
        objections to 9
        objections to, how taken 11
        presumption that all claims disposed of by 19

PAGE

Award, recitals in 21
    signing of 21,22, 36
    taking up 20
    time for making 36
        where submission in contract........ 58
        by order of Court.................. 59
    to be binding.............................. 40
    to be deposited with Registrar 36
    to be final settlement 40
    to be in writing.................................21, 36
Barristers, representation by.............. 36
Board of Trade, Council of, to determine number of Arbitra-
        tors 23
        rooms, etc., provided...................26, 53
        may make rules 47
        formation of, in cities other than Toronto.... 47
        electing members of, as Arbitrators....... . 25
Certificate may be filed.................................... 31
Chamber of arbitration, how established.................23, 24
        of Toronto, Rules of................ 51
          how constituted 51
          object of. 51
          officers of 51
Christian, Form of oath of.. 34
Collateral dispute between Arbitrator and party 10
Commission to take evidence 42
Consent of Arbitrator to act......... ....24, 52
Contract, submission in writing 57
Conveyance, award may direct 20
Copy of award, party may have.. 36
Corporations, submissions of to be under seal.. 7
Corroboration of evidence where estate of deceased person a
        party........................29, 30
Costs in discretion of arbitrator....................... 43
    may be lump sum 21
    of adjourned hearing 38
    of attendance of counsel.... 38
    of attendance of witnesses 44, 45
    f recovery of fees 46

PAGE

Costs, part of awai d 20
    registrar to receive 27, 56
    table of 45
    to be awarded separately 20
Council of Board may make rules 47
Counsel, assessor not to act as 61
    authority of, to be filed 38
    notice of presence of, to be given 38
    presence of 2, 13, 38
    to file authority 38
Court, Arbitration pursuant to order of.. 58
    may refer matters to Toronto Chamber of Arbitration 51
    opinion of, cannot be obtained..................... 39
Credit of witness may be impeached........................ 13
Crime, disqualification of Arbitrator by 25, 52
Cross examination of witnesses 13, 14
Death of Arbitrator 7, 59
    party 3, 29
Deceased person, evidence against estate of 29, 30
Declaration to be made by Arbitrators..................... 54
               form of 65
Deputy Registrar.. 57
Description of lands, etc., must be sufficient 22
Discretion, appointment of third Arbitrator an act of 55
Discretion of Arbitrator as to adjournment............... 37
               costs................ 43
               witness fees..............44, 45
Disqualification of Arbitrator by crime 25
Documents, production of..... .... 3, 32, 33
Enlargement of hearing................................. 37
        time for doing any act................. 6
        time for making award 36
Evidence, arbitrator not bound by strict rules of 13
    assessor may rule as to 3
    commission to take............................. 42
    examples of mode of taking........... 15
    must be received 14
    must be relevant 13
    not to be taken ex-parte........................ 14
    of foreign witness, costs of...................... 45
    order in which, given 15

PAGE

Evidence, party taken by surprise by 37

     rules of 13

     should be regularly before Arbitrator............ 40

     taken on commission........................... 42

     where estate of deceased person involved........29, 30

Examination of witnesses, rules as to 13, 14

Examples of mode of taking evidence...................... 15

Execution for fees where award not taken up............... 46

Ex-parte, application to Registrar may be 55

     evidence not to be taken 14

Expenses of attendance of counsel......................... 38

Experts as Arbitrators.................................... 24

Facts on which decision based need not be stated........... 22

Failure of Arbitrator to act..............................7, 59

Fees, recovery of 46

     of Arbitrators... 45

         where reference not included............ 54

     of assessor 62

     of witnesses............................. 43

     payable....................................2, 43, 45

     penalty for demanding more than legal............... 20

     recoverable although award not taken up............. 46

     registrar to receive 27, 56

     special agreement as to 45

     to be paid before copy of award handed out............ 36

Final, award must be 18

Form of award 20

Forms to be provided....................................26, 53

Forms :

     Application for appointment of third Arbitrator..... 69

         attendance of legal assessor......... 73

     Appointment of Arbitrator by Board of Trade...... 64

         Registrar............. 68

        third Arbitrator.................... 69

     Arbitrator's oath.... 49

        declaration 65, 67

     Assent to nomination as Arbitrator....... 64

     Declaration by Arbitrator...................... 65, 67

     Notice of reconciliation 70

     Notification of appointment of Arbitrators by parties 65

        third Arbitrator...... 66

		PAGE
Forms, Oath of Arbitrator		49
	Oath of witness	34, 49
	Request for attendance of legal assessor	73
	Submission	48,70,71, 72
	Summons to witness	50
Fraud, award may be set aside for		40
	form of reference where question of	8
	injunction where arbitrators guilty of	41
	motion to set aside award for	42
	will vitiate award, what	40
Future differences may be referred		8
	Form of reference of	8

General Arbitrations Act, I894:—

Synopsis of Act	1, 5	S. 19		38
S. 1	6	S. 20		38
S. 2	23	S. 21		39
S. 3 ss 1	25	S. 22		39
ss 2, 3, 4, 5, 6	26	S. 23		40
S. 4	26	S. 24		42
S. 5	27	S. 25		42
S. 6.	27	S. 26		42
S. 7	27	S. 27		43
S. 8	28	S. 28		43
S. 9	29	S. 29		45
S. 10	29	S. 30		45
S. 11	31	S. 31		46
S. 12	31	S. 32		47
S. 13	32	S. 33		47
S. 14	33	S. 34		47
S. 15	33	Schedule A	27, 48,	52
S. 16	36	" B	29,	49
S. 17	36	" C	34,	49
S. 18	37	" D	32,	50

		PAGE
Hearing, adjournment of		37
	all arbitrators to attend	45
	costs of adjourned	38
	neglect of arbitrator to attend	45
	notice of	27, 43, 56
	adjourned	37
	time of	37
	to be continued *de die in diem*	37
	who may attend	39

PAGE

Holidays, office closed on 56
    non included in computation of time, when 62
    time expiring on 62
Incompetency of arbitrator, crime a cause of 41
    injunction in case of............... 41
Inconsistent with Act, rules not to be.................... 47
Indemnity, form of reference as to 41
Infant, submission by 7
Injunction, Court may interfere by....................11, 41
    prevention of injustice by 41, 42
    takes place of leave to revoke submission........ 12
    where Arbitrator incompetent................. 41
Interest in result, Arbitrator must not have 10, 41
Jew, oath of 34
Judge may refer matter to Toronto Chamber of Arbitration... 51
Jurisdiction, Arbitrator exceeding........................ 41
    of Toronto Chamber of Arbitration..... 51
Land, Form of reference as to title to.................... 41
Law,   "   "   "   questions of.................. 41
Leading Questions, Witness not to be asked............... 13
Legal assessor... 3
    appointment of........................... 61
    how attendance of, procured.................. 61
    not to act as counsel....................... 62
    request for attendance of, form 73
List of Arbitrators to be posted up and published 25
    selection of Arbitrators from..........53, 60
Lump sum, Arbitrator may award.......................... 19
Lunatic, submission by 7
Majority of Arbitrators may sign award................... 45
Manager of litigant company as Arbitrator................ 11
Matters to be referred................................... 8
Menonist, Oath of....................................... 34
Money award must be exact.... 22
Moravian, Oath of,..... 35
Names of Arbitrators to be posted and published........... 25
Notes, Arbitrator should take............................ 17
Notice, enlargement of time for giving 60
    how served................................ 55
    of adjourned hearing.......... 37
    of appointment of Arbitrator by parties............. 65

PAGE

Notice of attendance of agent, etc., to be given 38

    of election to be sent to Arbitrators 52, 54, 56

    of hearing, length of. 43

        to be given......................27, 43, 56

    reconciliation, Form of. 69

Number of parties to arbitration... 7

    Arbitrators......... ....23, 27, 53

Oath, Affirmation instead of...................... ....33, 35

    form of 34

    omission to take 29

    of Arbitrator....................... ....28, 29

        form of................................. 49

    witness....................................... 3, 33, 34

        form of 34, 49

Objection to award, how taken 11

    on ground that Arbitrator not sworn..... 29

    what is 9

Office closed on holidays............................ 56

Office fees to be paid 43

    what 45

    of Toronto Chamber of Arbitration... 51

Officers   "   "   "   56

Opinion of Court, Arbitrator cannot obtain................ 39

Order of Court, Arbitration pursuant to... 58

    submission after 59

Papers to be provided............................26, 33, 53

Parties, Attendance of, may be dispensed with............3, 39

    may agree on Arbitrator...................... 53

    request attendance of assessor......... 61

    to Arbitration........................ 7

    to be given notice of hearing..... 56

    to pay fees in equal shares, when 54

Partners, reference in case of disputes between 8

    submission of 7

Party, absence of 3, 33

    death of 3, 29

    begins, which 15

    may conduct his own case 2

    have copy of award............................ 36

    travelling expenses of, allowed, when.................. 44

PAGE

Perjury..34, 36
Post, notices may be served by 55
Presumption that Arbitrator had disposed of all claims...... 19
Private, proceedings to be........................... ......2, 39
Privilege, claim of 32
Procedure, general remarks on 2
    in cases not specifically provided for.............. 42
    order of 14
    where party does not attend..................... 3
Proceedings to be private.............................2, 39
Production of documents...........................3, 33
    privilege to refuse 32
    summons for 27, 32
Publicatiom of list of Arbitrators.................... 25
    report of proceedings not allowed... 2
Quaker, oath of.. 34
Reasons, Arbitrator need not state 22
Recitals in award.. 21
Reconciliation, agreement of 61
    form of notice of..................... 69
    register to be kept.................. . ..27,56, 61
Re-examination of witness............................ 14
Reference, Arbitrator regulates order of business on........,.. 17
    by order of Court............. 58
    form of 8, 40
    not concluded, Fees of Arbitrators where......... 54
    order of business on 14
    scope of 8, 40
    to be clearly stated..................... 8
    to Toronto Chamber of Arbitration, voluntary 51
    by order of Court 51
Refusal of Arbitrator to act............................ 7, 59
Register of Awards and Reconciliations................27,56, 61
    submissions 27, 56
Registrar, absence of 57
    application to, may be ex-parte 55
    appoint new Arbitrator......................... 60
    deputy of 57
    duties of 27, 56
    fees of 43, 45
    gives notice of hearing......................... 43

PAGE

Registrar issues summons for attendance of witness. 32
      production of document........ 32
   makes returns...............................27, 56
   may extend time.................................. 60
   notifies Arbitrator of election.................... 52
   " party of attendance of counsel. 38
   Secretary of Board of Trade to be.............27, 56
   selects Arbitrator................................ 53
Regulations must be consistent with Act.................... 47
   to be made by Board of Trade........... 47
Reporters, presence of 39
Reports of proceedings not to be issued.................... 2
Returns, Registrar to make.................. ....27, 56
Revocation of Submission........... ....1?, 27, 28
  " " " not affected by death of party...... 29
Rooms to be provided.............. . ...26, 53
Rule of Court, making award 31
Rules, alterations of 63
   must be consistent with Act........................ 47
   of Toronto Chamber of Arbitrarion................. 51
   to be made by Board of Trade........ 47
   where reference by order of Court................... 59
Schedule of fees..43, 44
Secretary of Board of Trade to be officer of Toronto Chamber
  of Arbitration................................. 56
Secretary of Board of Trade to be Registrar.............27, 56
Service of notices may be by post................. 55
Setting aside award...................................... 40
Short title of Act......... 6
Sick person, evidence of 42
Signature of all Arbitrators to be at same time........... 21, 22
Signing award... 36
Solicitor, attendance of 2, 38
   notice of attendance of 38
   to file authority. 38
Special fees, agreement as to 45
Stated case...3, 39
Submission, after agreement in written contract..........57, 58
   " order of Court.......... ... .58, 59
   by Agent, effect of 7
   " infant, " " 7

PAGE

Submission by lunatic, effect of 7
   contained in written contract.................... 57
   effect of death of party on 3
   form of 48, 57, 62, 71, 72
   irrevocable..................................... 2, 29
   may be filed with award......................... 31
   may be made a rule of court 31
   of corporation................................. 7
   of partners 7
   registrar to receive 27, 56
   revocation of 12, 27
   sole basis of Arbitrator's authority............. 9
   to be in writing............................... 57
   where arbitration between members of Board of Trade.... 47
   where dispute between partners................. 8
Submissions, register of, to be kept 27, 56
Subpœna, not necessary......................... 32
Subsidiary questions, determination of........... 40
Summons, disobedience to....................... 32
   to witness................................... 34
   form of..................................... 50
Sunday, office closed on........................ 56
   not included in computation of time, where........ 62
   time expiring on 62
Surprise of party a reason for adjournment.......... 37
Surveyor as witness, fees of..................... 44
Taking up award................................ 20
Technical phraseology unnecessary................ 21
Third Arbitrator, application for appointment of, Form of .. 69
   appointment of 53, 55, 56
Third Arbitrator, form of appointment of, by arbitrators.... 69
   form of modification of appointment of..... 66
Time, enlargement of........................... 60
   for making award............................ 36
   after reference by order of court.... 59
   for making award after submission in contract........ 58
   for moving against award..................... 42
   how reckoned................................ 62
   of hearing.................................. 37
   of notice of hearing......................... 43

PAGE

Title of Act 6

Toronto Board of Trade, Secretary of, to be officer of Toronto
    Chamber of Arbitration 56

      Board of Trade, Secretary of, to be Registrar 27, 56

Toronto Chamber of Arbitration, how constituted 51

                   objects of 51

                   office of 51

                   officers of 56

                   rules of 51

Travelling expenses of party 44

              witness............................. 44

Tunker, oath of 34

Umpire, improperly appointed 55, 56

    to be notified of appointment..................... 27

Unprovided for cases, law applicable to 42

Voluntary reference to Toronto Chamber of Arbitration 51

Voluntary Submissions, law of, applied.................... 42

Witness, absence of, a ground for adjournment............. 37

    credit of, may be impeached 13

    examination of 13

    fees of 43

    foreign, costs of procuring attendance of 45

    may be convicted of perjury...................34, 36

    oath of 34, 49

    re-examination of 14

    summons to 27, 32, 50

    to award unnecessary 21

    to be sworn 3, 33, 34

    travelling expenses of 44

    who disobeys summons............. 32

Witnesses, commission to examine......................... 42

Writing, agreement to pay special fees to be in 45

    award to be in 21, 36

    consent of arbitrator to act to be in 24, 52

    enlargement of time for making award to be in..... 36

    submission to be in 57

Written contract, arbitration after submission in 58

    submission in........................... 57

www.ingramcontent.com/pod-product-compliance
Lightning Source LLC
Chambersburg PA
CBHW032247080426
42735CB00008B/1037